# NORDIC WINTER KNITS

Maja Karlsson

AF729771

# NORDIC WINTER KNITS

Maja Karlsson

PHOTOGRAPHY: HELÉN PE

BATSFORD

## Patterns

# Foreword

The winter I wrote this book turned out to be the longest and coldest in living memory in Värmland, where I live. The snow had already settled in November, and lingered long into April. The hoarfrost embroidered roses on the windows and the snowflakes danced around the corners of the house. It was as if King Bore himself wanted to teach me something about the very nature of winter. Every day that passed I immersed myself deeper into the reality of winter life and in earnest experienced what long-lasting cold means. There were many fires in the wood burner and double layers of woolly socks on the feet. Once again, I was reminded what an important part of winter's rhythm knitted garments are.

This book is here to help knitters create their own winter wardrobe. You will find hats, scarves, cardigans and jumpers, as well as mittens, socks and more. A few old friends also make an appearance, such as a hat version of my now classic pattern, Sisterhood, and also my famous hotpants Maja's Mamelucker – now in multiple sizes. Some garments are winter warm and will help you keep warm outdoors, others are cooler and will work well indoors or as one of several warming layers. The wool garments can be combined in an infinite number of ways or be worn separately. They are knitted using techniques including colourwork, cables and lace. Are you new to knitting? If so, I warmly recommend the Arctic set, that includes three beginner-friendly garments.

*Nordic Winter Knits* is also a journey through the winter months. We begin in October at Michaelmas, the starting point of winter according to the old Farmer's Almanac. Then we experience Lucia with candles in her hair, a festive advent calendar, Christmas celebration with colourful paper flowers and pine branches, a joyful Christmas morning and socks with Christmas trees. We greet the new year with a jumper called just January before we land in a beautiful late-winter Valentine's Day celebration.

We visit the ancient farm Karlsgården in Hälsingland and gaze out at mountains and valleys. Thereafter we dream ourselves away to Norway, the Arctic and the frozen tundra. On the way we meet two little cats and a dappled grey horse. It feels extra nice to let the animals take up room in my book. There's also room for a dash of black magic and a stargazing map with the glimmering star signs of the Milky Way.

Welcome into my winter dream of knitting! I hope you will feel at home and that you'll find your favourite garment to knit that will follow you for many years to come. Perhaps you will lose yourself in the world of colourwork, or let yourself be charmed by a calm, winter white jumper? Regardless of what you choose to knit, I wish you many happy moments in company with this book, written to spread warmth in the winter cold.

*Warm regards,*
*Maja*

*Arvika, April 2024*

# About winter knitting

Knitting in the winter comes to me as naturally as bringing in wood and lighting a fire. That can of course be due to me often being freezing cold – I actually feel the cold more than anyone else I know, and therefore I always long for warmth. Perhaps that's why I wanted to create a book full with garments that warm frozen winter souls so much?

Warmth can come in different forms: a pair of colourwork mittens, a hug, or a cat that purrs. Reading a poem in the evenings also bring warmth. This one is written by Gustaf Fröding, and it is so beautiful:

> 'Don't be sad though the clouds are heavy
> and winter's cold runs through the heart.
> For behind clouds shines sun and happiness
> and after winter spring will come again.'

My most intense knitting period is usually between October and March. It's as if the hands come to life when everything else is still. The winter evenings suddenly have a purpose and meaning thanks to the knitting. Creating our own clothes brings such satisfaction.

In Sweden, we have been knitting since the 17th century. One exciting fact is that the further north in the country we get, the more common it was to knit colourwork patterns with multiple threads, which of course also makes the garments warmer. In Värmland, where I live, there's a tradition to knit very beautiful colourwork mittens. When I design knitting patterns, I usually take that tradition as my starting point. I like to create new patterns that build on old motifs.

In this book you'll find several colourwork garments. For example, the Selbu-inspired hat Sisterhood, which is included in a collection of garments that I have made with the same important message and motif: we are not alone – there is always a hand to hold. Here is also the pattern for Christmas Day, the collared mittens that, among other things, are adorned with a leaf tendril – a type of pattern that I've always admired.

If you like stars, I want to highlight the Nore slippers, which are a celebration of our neighbouring country Norway, or the Wolf Winter mittens, which are among the warmest you can wear. And don't miss Black Magic, my masterpiece – a cardigan that I have wanted to make for a long time and is inspired by ancient symbols with supernatural powers.

If the cold is tough to those of us who live in the north, warm garments are what saves us. This is proven again and again. A winter from a long time ago comes to mind when the snowflakes fell softly outside the window and I gave birth to my daughter – my winter baby. In the bag I brought to the hospital were newly knitted little garments, filled with warmth and love in abundance. To warm another person is the best thing ever. I hope that *Nordic Winter Knits* will inspire you to do the same!

In the end love is the only thing that matters. I even made a jumper with that name, you'll find it on p147. Let it remind you of what is the greatest and what will always come first.

But now, let's get going, shall we? Take out your knitting needles and yarn. Let us warm each other with winter knits!

# Before you start

The patterns are sorted into three levels of difficulty:

1 = Easy 2 = Intermediate 3 = Advanced

If you are a beginner knitter, I recommend the Arctic collection on p59. Those garments are specially designed to be beginner-friendly. That also goes for the January jumper on p139.

The garments in the book are sized according to women's clothes sizes. To decide the size for your cardigan or jumper, you will need to measure your chest. Then add desired positive ease and compare the measurement with the measurement of the finished cardigan. Then pick the size that is closest to your total measurement. Read more about sizing on p154 in the Knitting School.

Keep in mind that you can always lengthen or shorten the body and sleeves on cardigans and jumpers, if you wish. If you lengthen it, you will however need more yarn than what's specified in the pattern.

To decide which sock size to knit, you might have to measure your foot using a tape measure. Here's how: measure the circumference of the widest part of your foot (= the circumference of the sock), then measure the length of your foot from toe to heel (= size). Keep in mind that all socks are stretchy. An unstretched sock that measures 1–1.5 cm (0.4–0.6in) shorter than your foot length will have a good fit. NB: the length of the leg is always measured from the end of the heel.

Read through the whole pattern description before you start knitting to get an idea of the construction and the method.

For information about abbreviations, see p158.

All measurements in centimetres and inches are approximate.

The yarn usage specified in the patterns refers in most cases to whole balls/skeins needed, and not the actual usage, which can sometimes be less.

I recommend knitting a test swatch before you start knitting the actual garment. This is to check that your tension is correct. Make the test swatch approximately 12 x 12cm (4 ¾ x 4 ¾ in). Count the number of stitches and rows you get over 10 x 10cm (4 x 4in). If your tension is out – change knitting needle size. Do you have too few stitches per row? Change to smaller needles. Do you have too many stitches per row? Change to larger needles.

If you can't find the yarn that's listed, you can substitute it with a yarn of the same material and equivalent tension.

# Michaelmas

Michaelmas is celebrated on the first Sunday in October. Historically, it was one of the biggest holidays in the farming community – when markets and harvest feasts took place, weddings were celebrated and servants were given time off or could change employer. Michaelmas marked the turn from summer to winter. The growing season was wrapped up, the animals were brought inside and the light summer clothes were replaced by warm winter clothes.

With the Michaelmas mittens, you can welcome winter! They are rustic and warm, and have a folkloric harvest design on the cuffs. The magnificent flower stem symbolises the bounty that humans throughout time have felt when the harvest has been brought in.

YARN: Léttlopi from Ístex – 100% Icelandic wool, 50g (1.8oz) = 100m (110yd)

TENSION: 22 sts × 26 rows in stocking stitch using 4mm needles = 10 × 10cm (4 × 4in)

SIZES: One size – women's

MITTEN WIDTH: 10cm (4in)

MITTEN LENGTH: 25cm (9 ¾in)

AMOUNTS: Colour 1 = 100g (3.5oz) Light Beige Heather (no. 0086), colour 2 = 20g (0.7oz) Black Sheep Heather (no. 0052), colour 3 = small amount of Rust Heather (no. 9427)

DOUBLE-POINTED NEEDLES: 3.5mm and 4mm

DIFFICULTY LEVEL: 2 of 3

CONSTRUCTION: The mittens are knit from the bottom up, with increases for a thumb gusset and a colourwork cuff that starts with a Latvian braid.

TECHNIQUES: M1B = increase 1 st in the stitch below. See Knitting School, p159.

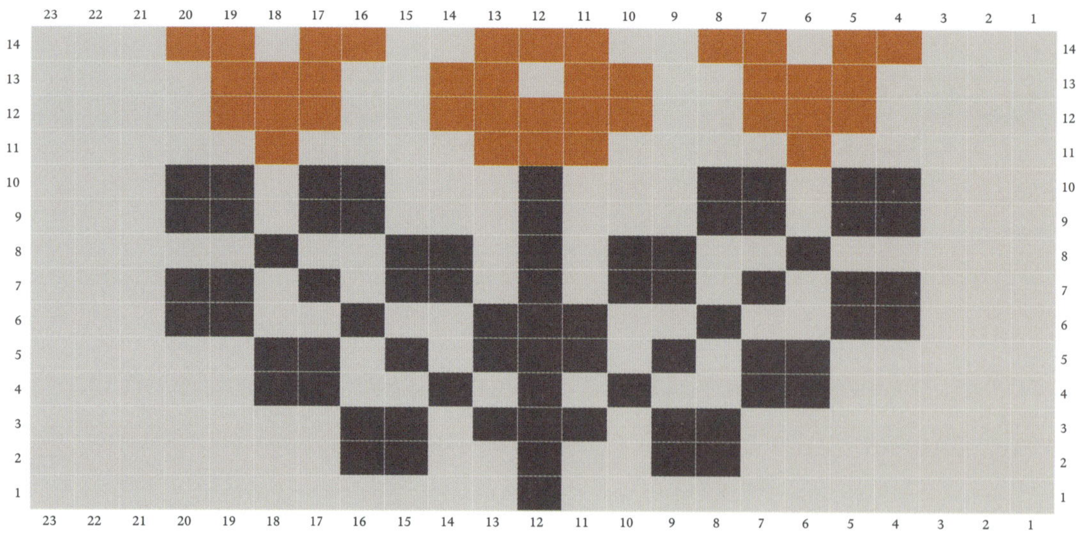


## RIGHT MITTEN

With 4mm dpns and colour 2, cast on 46 sts and divide them evenly over four needles (= 12 + 11 + 12 + 11 sts).

*Latvian braid*

See p160 in the Knitting School.

ROUND 1: *K1 with colour 2, k1 with colour 3*, repeat from *–* to end of round.

ROUND 2: *P1 with colour 2, p1 with colour 3*, repeat from *–* to end of round. NB: hold both threads at the front of the work while knitting. For each colour change the new yarn should go *under* the yarn you just knitted with.

ROUND 3: *p1 with colour 2, p1 with colour 3*, repeat from *–* to end of round. NB: hold both threads at the front of the work while knitting. For each colour change the new yarn should go *over* the yarn you just knitted with.

Knit 2 rounds with colour 1.

Knit in the round in stocking stitch (= knit all stitches when working in the round) and knit colourwork pattern following the chart (repeat stitches 1–23, 2 times per round for 14 rounds).

Change to 3.5mm dpns and colour 1 and knit 4 rounds.

*Thumb gusset*

INCREASE ROUND 1: Knit until you reach needle 3, M1B (see Techniques) in the $3^{rd}$ and $5^{th}$ st. Knit to end of round and then knit 1 round without increases.

INCREASE ROUND 2: Knit until you reach needle 3, M1B in the $3^{rd}$ and $7^{th}$ st. Knit to end of round and then knit 1 round without any increases.

INCREASE ROUND 3: Knit until you reach needle 3, M1B in the $3^{rd}$ and $9^{th}$ st. Knit to end of round and then knit 1 round without any increases.

INCREASE ROUND 4: Knit until you reach needle 3, M1B in the $3^{rd}$ and $11^{th}$ st. Knit to end of round and then knit 1 round without any increases.

INCREASE ROUND 5: Knit until you reach needle 3, M1B in the $3^{rd}$ and $13^{th}$ st. Knit to end of round and then knit 1 round without any increases.

INCREASE ROUND 6: Knit until you reach needle 3, M1B in the $3^{rd}$ and $15^{th}$ st. Knit to end of round and then knit 1 round without any increases. Knit 25 sts, transfer the 15 sts from the thumb gusset to a stitch holder or a length of scrap yarn.

*Continue the hand*

Cast on 3 new stitches 'behind' the thumb using the double twisted loop technique (see video links in the Knitting School on p160) and knit to end of round.

Work in stocking stitch for 8cm (3 ¼in).

DECREASE ROUND FOR TOP OF MITTEN: K1, SL1, k1 and pass the slipped st over the one you've just knitted. Knit to last 3 sts on needle 2: k2tog, k1. Needle 3: k1, SL1, k1 and pass the slipped st over the one you've just knitted. Knit to last 3 st on needle 4: k2tog, k1 = 4 sts decreased.

Repeat the decrease round every other row 2 times, and then every round until 10 sts remain.

Cut the yarn and pass through the remaining stitches. Pull tightly and secure the yarn.

*Thumb*

With 3.5mm dpns and colour 1, divide the 15 thumb stitches over four dpns, and pick up 3 new stitches in the previously cast on stitches 'behind' the thumb = 18 sts. Knit in the round until the thumb measures 5.5cm (2 ¼in).

Work the decrease round as for the hand, but working it each round until 10 sts remain.

Cut the yarn and pass through the remaining stitches. Pull tightly and secure the yarn.

*Left mitten*

Knit as for right mitten, but start the thumb gusset in the 3rd and 5th stitch from the end of needle 4. Then increase as for the right mitten, but count from the end of needle 4 instead of the beginning of needle 3.

# Nore

Nore is an Old Norse name that is sometimes used as a personification of our neighbouring country Norway. I live close to the Norwegian border and share a lot of the knitting tradition found on the borderland between Sweden and Norway.

The Nore slippers are a celebration of all the skilful Norwegian knitters I have had the pleasure of meeting over the years. They are adorned with the eight-petal rose motifs which both our knitting traditions share. These slippers are great as guest slippers, a Christmas present or even as a gift for a good neighbour.

YARN: Svensk Ull 3 tr – 100% wool, 100g (3.5oz) = 180m (197yd)

TENSION: 18 sts × 24 rows in stocking stitch in pattern using 4.5mm needles = 10 × 10cm (4 × 4in)

SIZE: One size – women's UK 5-7/EU 38-40

SLIPPER LENGTH: 25cm (9 ¾in)

SLIPPER WIDTH: 10cm (4in)

AMOUNTS: Colour 1 = 50g (1.8oz) Pine Tree Green (no. 59008), colour 2 = 50g (1.8oz) Wasa Crisp (no. 59021)

DOUBLE-POINTED NEEDLES: 4mm and 4.5mm

DIFFICULTY LEVEL: 2 of 3

CONSTRUCTION: The slipper is knit from the toe up.

TECHNIQUES: Judy's magic cast on, see video links in the Knitting School on p160.

M1L = increase 1 st slanting left, see Knitting School, p159.

M1R = increase 1 st slanting right, see Knitting School, p159.

## SLIPPER

With two 4.5mm dpns and colour 1, cast on 20 sts using Judy's magic cast on technique (see Techniques). Divide the stitches evenly over four needles and join to knit in the round.

ROUND 1: Knit.

ROUND 2: K1, M1L (see Techniques), k8, M1R (see Techniques), k1, k1, M1L, k8, M1R, k1 = 24 sts.

ROUNDS 3, 5, 7 AND 9: Knit.

ROUND 4: K1, M1L, k10, M1R, k1, k1, M1L, k10, M1R, k1 = 28 sts.

ROUND 6: K1, M1L, k12, M1R, k1, k1, M1L, k12, M1R, k1 = 32 sts.

ROUND 8: K1, M1L, k14, M1R, k1, k1, M1L, k14, M1R, k1 = 36 sts.

ROUND 10: K1, M1L, k16, M1R, k1, k1, M1L, k16, M1R, k1 = 40 sts.

ROUND 11: Knit to end of round.

Knit the pattern following chart A, rounds 1–25 (stitches 1–40).

Change to 4mm dpns and colour 1 and work 4 rows in garter stitch back and forth over the stitches on the first two dpns. Then cast off these stitches.

With 4mm dpns, cast on 20 new stitches. Work 3 rows in garter stitch back and forth. The new stitches correspond to the stitches on the first two needles when knitting in the round.

Change to 4.5mm dpns and return to knitting in the round and work pattern and decreases following chart B. Cast off.

## FINISHING

Sew the heel together on the inside of the cast-off edge. Sew together the garter stitch side edges: Place edge over edge and sew through both layers. Weave in loose ends. Knit the second slipper the same way.

CHART A

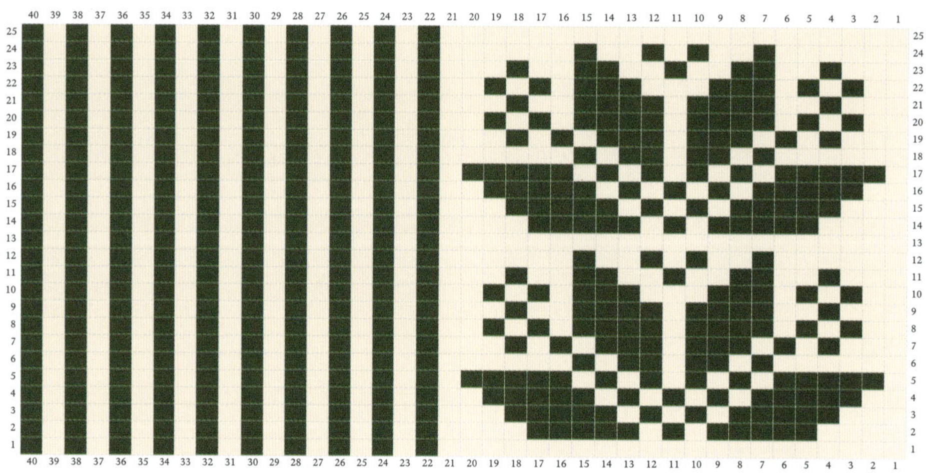

CHART B

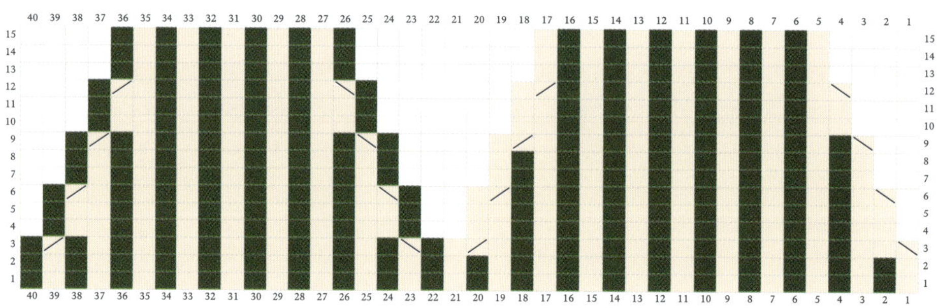

⟍ Slip 1 st, k1, pass the slipped st over the one you've just knitted ⟋ K2tog No stitch

NORDEN BL. 4
NORGE

# Fimbul

In Norse mythology, the Fimbulwinter is a long and cold period that signifies the end of the world.

It is said that the Fimbulwinter would last for three years without any summer between. Snowstorms would then sweep across the ice-covered world and, in pure desperation, humans would start wars with each other. Eventually, the Fenris wolf would devour the sun and the stars would fall from their places, the sky turning dark.

The Fimbul scarf is knitted with one strand mohair tweed and one strand mohair silk with a nice sheen. You can wrap it around yourself during dark winter evenings or curl up underneath it together with someone you want to warm up.

YARN: No 1 – Mohair Tweed from Järbo, 70% merino wool, 30% mohair, 50g (1.8oz) = 110m (120yd) and Fin Mohair Silke from Järbo, 72% mohair, 28% silk, 25g (0.9oz) = 210m (230yd)

TENSION: 17 sts × 36 rows in garter stitch using 4.5mm needles = 10 × 10cm (4 × 4in)

SIZE: One size

SCARF WIDTH: 144cm (57in) from point to point

SCARF HEIGHT: 58cm (23in)

AMOUNTS: Colour 1 = 300g (10.6oz) Mohair Tweed (no. 22306, Vanilla Shortbread), colour 2 = 100g (3.5oz) Fin Mohair Silke (no. 31524, Almondine)

CIRCULAR NEEDLES: 4.5mm, 120cm (47in) long

DIFFICULTY LEVEL: 3 of 3

CONSTRUCTION: The scarf is knit in rows from the bottom point, then stitches are picked up along one edge at a time to work the edging.

TECHNIQUES: Double chain cast off = *yo, p1 but loop the yarn clockwise around the needle when purling. Pass the yo over the first stitch on the right needle. Pass the second stitch over the first stitch on the right needle.* Repeat from *–* until all stitches have been cast off. See also video links in the Knitting School, p160.

NB: the whole scarf is knitted with one strand of colour 1 and one strand of colour 2 at the same time (= 2 strands in total).

### TRIANGLE SCARF

Cast on 2 sts.

ROW 1: K1, yo, k1 = 3 sts.

ROW 2: SL1 purlwise (i.e. with yarn in front of work), k1, yo, k1 = 4 sts.

ROW 3: SL1 purlwise (i.e. with yarn in front of work), knit to last st on the needle, yo, k1 = 1 st increased.

Repeat row 3 until you have 193 sts on the needle. (97 'holes' should have formed on each side of the scarf).

Cast off the scarf using the double chain cast off technique (see Techniques). Weave in loose ends.

### EDGING A

With the right side facing you, pick up 1 st in each 'hole' along the scarf's left slanted edge = 97 sts. When all stitches have been picked up, cast on a further 9 new stitches on the needle. Turn and work the edging as follows.

ROW 1: *K1, p1*, repeat from *–* once more, k5. Place yarn in front of the work, transfer the next stitch, that was picked up along the edge of the scarf, to the right needle, turn.

ROW 2: K2tog (i.e. the transferred stitch is knitted together with the edge stitch), k2, *k2tog, yo*. Repeat from *–* once more, k1, yo, k1, turn.

ROW 3: *K1, p1*, repeat from *–* twice more, k4. Place yarn in front of the work, transfer the next stitch, that was picked up along the edge of the scarf, to the right needle, turn. NB: for all odd rows that follow, the row is finished with the yarn placed in front of work and a picked-up stitch from the scarf is transferred to the right needle, turn.

ROW 4: K2tog, k1, *k2tog, yo*, repeat from *–* once more, k3, yo, k1, turn.

ROW 5: K1, p1, k3, p1, k1, p1, k3.

ROW 6: K2tog, *k2tog, yo*, repeat from *–* once more, k5, yo, k1, turn.

ROW 7: K1, p1, k5, p1, k1, p1, k2.

ROW 8: K2tog, k2, *yo, k2tog*, repeat from *–* once more, k1, k2tog, yo, k2tog, turn.

ROW 9: K1, p1, k3, p1, k1, p1, k3.

ROW 10: K2tog, k3, yo, k2tog, yo, k3tog, yo, k2tog, turn.

ROW 11: *K1, p1*, repeat from *–* twice more, k4.

ROW 12: K2tog, k4, yo, k3tog, yo, k2tog, turn.

ROW 13: *K1, p1*, repeat from *–* once more, k5.

Repeat rows 2–13 until all picked-up stitches along the left edge have been worked. The final repetition is finished with row 13, then cast off the remaining 9 sts.

### EDGING B

With the right side facing you, pick up 1 st in each 'hole' along the scarf's right slanted edge. When all stitches have been picked up, cast on a further 9 new stitches on the needle. Turn and work lace edging as for Edging A.

### FINISHING

Weave in loose ends. Block the scarf carefully to the measurements specified and instructions in the Knitting School, p156.

Make sure to pin down the edges of the scarf when blocking to make the lace pattern stand out.

# Advent

Various kinds of Christmas tablecloths were my inspiration for the Advent socks. Woven, embroidered and printed – often with red pattern designs on a white or linen-coloured base.

In my large Värmland cabinet I have a drawer with large and small Christmas tablecloths. My grandma embroidered many of them, including beautiful little runners for the windowsills. There are also the star-shaped tablecloths my other grandma sewed.

The Advent sock is a form of Advent calendar. The pattern is divided into four parts, so if you have two socks on the go at the same time and knit one part for each Advent Sunday, you will have a finished pair of festive socks just in time for Christmas!

YARN: Junior Raggi from Järbo, 75% superwash wool, 25% polyamide, 50g (1.8oz) = 200m (219yd)

TENSION: 36 sts × 48 rows in stocking stitch in pattern with 3mm needles = 10 × 10cm (4 × 4in)

SIZES: UK 3/4 (5/6) 7/8 / EU 36/37 (38/39) 40/41

SOCK CIRCUMFERENCE: 18cm (7in)

SOCK LENGTH: 23–23.5 (24.5–25) 26–26.5cm / 9–9 ¼ (9 ½–9 ¾) 10 ¼–10 ½in

AMOUNTS: Colour 1 = 100g (3.5oz) Barley (no. 68425), colour 2 = 50g (1.8oz) Warm Red (no. 68406)

DOUBLE-POINTED NEEDLES: 2.5mm and 3mm

NOTIONS: 4 stitch markers

DIFFICULTY LEVEL: 3 of 3

CONSTRUCTION: The sock is knitted from the toe up with a ribbed classic heel for toe-up socks. Both the foot and the leg have elements of colourwork and the leg is finished with a ribbed cuff.

TECHNIQUES: M1L = increase 1 st slanting left, see Knitting School, p159.

M1R = increase 1 st slanting right, see Knitting School, p159.

Short rows and wrap and turn = see Knitting School, p158.

Judy's magic cast on, see video links in the Knitting School on p160.

*First week of Advent*

### TOE

With 2.5mm dpns and colour 1, cast on 24 sts over two needles (= 12 sts per needle) using Judy's magic cast on technique (see Techniques).

ROUND 1: Knit and at the same time, divide the stitches evenly over four needles.

ROUND 2: K1, M1L, knit to last st on needle 2, M1R, k1. Needle 3: K1, M1L, knit to last st on needle 4, M1R, k1.

Repeat rounds 1 and 2 until there are 64 sts. Stitches 1–32 = top, stitches 33–64 = bottom.

Knit 1 more round.

### FOOT

Sizes 3/4 and 5/6: knit colourwork pattern in stocking stitch (= knit every row when knitting in the round) following chart A1, rounds 1–31 (stitches 1–64).

Size 7/8: Knit colourwork pattern in stocking stitch (= knit every row when knitting in the round) following chart A2, rounds 1–39 (stitches 1–64).

With colour 1: Continue working in stocking stitch until the sock measures 13.5, 14.5, 15.5 cm (5 ¼, 5 ¾, 6in).

*Second week of Advent*

### GUSSET

ROUND 1: Top: Knit. Bottom: K1, M1L, knit to last st, M1R, k1.

ROUND 2: Knit.

Repeat rounds 1 –2 until you have 52 sts at the bottom.

Knit 1 round, and then the stitches across the top once. Now it's time to knit the heel.

### HEEL

The heel is knitted back and forth using short rows and wrapped stitches. Read about short rows and wrap and turn on p158 in the Knitting School. Now we only work with the stitches at the bottom/back. Place 4 stitch markers as follows: M1 after the 10th st, M2 after the 20th st, M3 after the 32nd st, M4 after the 42nd st.

Between M1 and M4 you have the middle 32 sts that will later become the heel flap.

Between M2 and M3 you have the middle 12 sts that will become centre back of the heel tip.

ROW 1 (RS): Knit to last st before M4, wrap and turn.

ROW 2 (WS): Purl to last st before M1, wrap and turn.

ROW 3 (RS): Knit to last st before the turn stitch from the previous row, wrap and turn.

ROW 4 (WS): Purl to last st before the turn stitch from the previous row, wrap and turn.

Repeat rows 3 and 4 until all stitches outside M2 and M3 are wrapped. The middle 12 sts in between M2 and M3 should not be wrapped.

NEXT ROW (RS): K12. Knit all wrapped stitches following the description for knit rows on p158 to M4. Turn.

NEXT ROW (WS): SL1 purlwise, purl until you reach the wrapped stitches (after M2). Purl all wrapped stitches following the description for purl rows on p158 to M1.

### HEEL FLAP

At the same time as the ribbed heel flap in the middle is worked, it should be joined together with the surrounding stitches (the heel gusset).

ROW 1 (RS): Turn and SL1 knitwise at the same time as you hold the yarn taut, p2. Work in k2, p2 rib until 1 st remains before M4, remove the stitch marker, k2tog tbl.

ROW 2 (WS): Turn and SL1 purlwise at the same time as you hold the yarn taut, k2. Work in p2, k2 rib to last st before M1, remove the stitch marker, p2tog. Remove the remaining stitch markers.

ROW 3 (RS): Turn and SL1 knitwise (hold yarn taut), work in rib to the slipped stitch. Knit the slipped stitch together with the next stitch from the heel gusset: K2tog tbl (= 1 st before + 1 st after the small 'gap' that has formed at the turning).

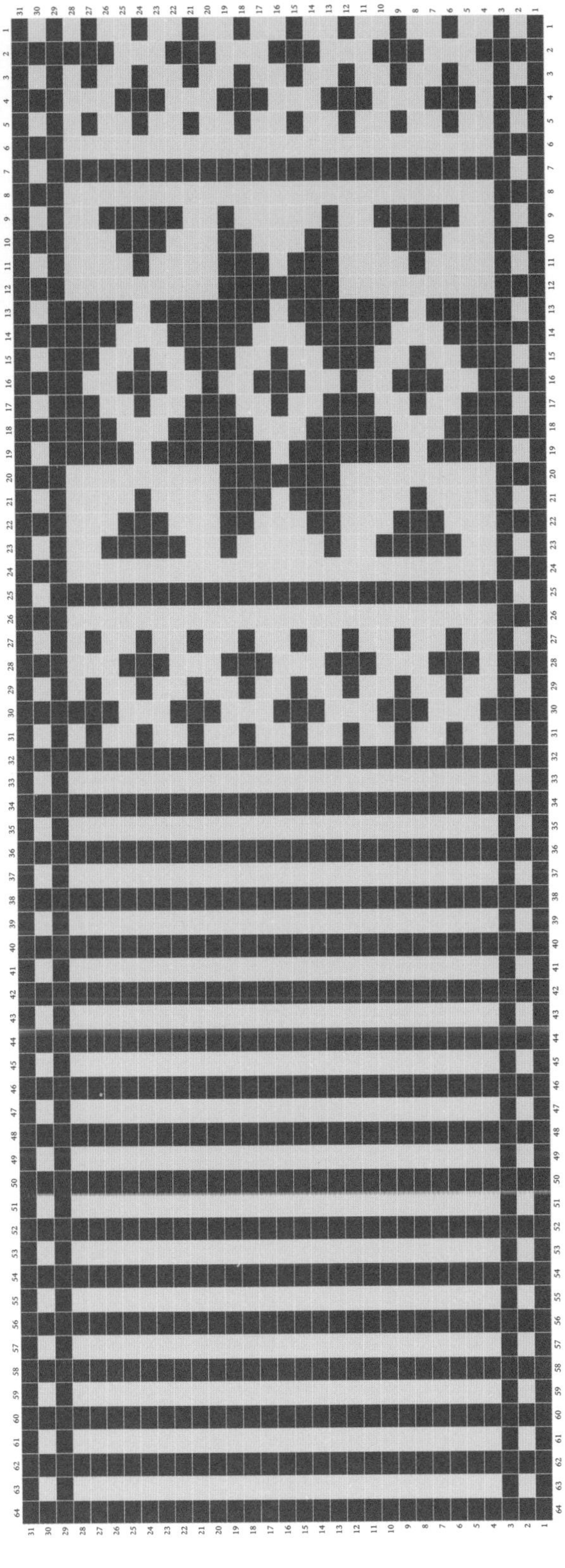

CHART A1

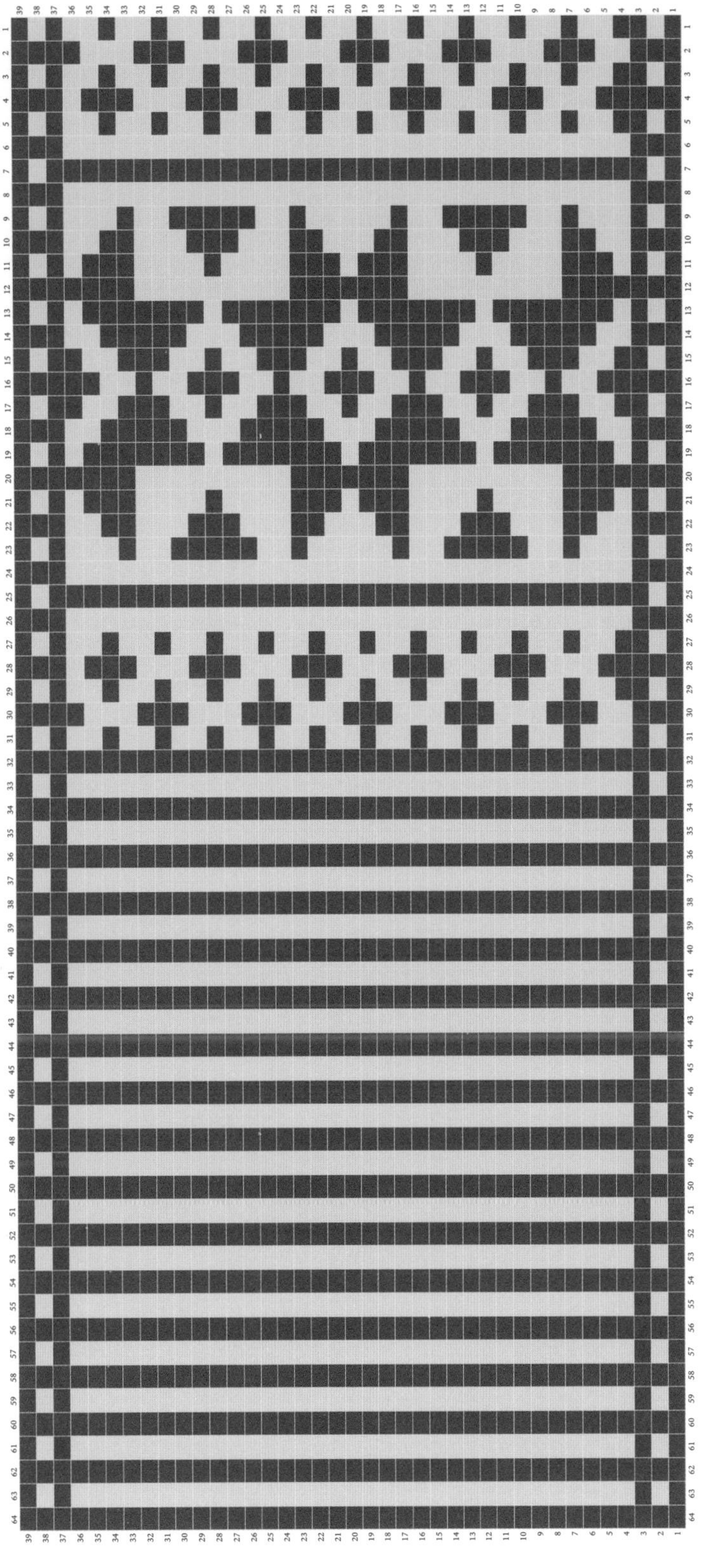

CHART A2

ROW 4 (WS): Turn and SL1 purlwise (hold yarn taut), work in rib to the slipped stitch. Purl the slipped stitch together with the next stitch from the heel gusset: P2tog (= 1 st before + 1 st after the 'gap').

Repeat rows 3–4 until you run out of gusset stitches (ending on a right-side row). Knit to end of row.

NEXT ROW: Top: Knit. Bottom: K2tog, work 31 sts in rib as before. You will now have the same number of stitches that you started with. The heel is finished!

*Third week of Advent*

### LEG

Work 20 rounds, working stocking stitch on the top and rib at the bottom.

Knit 2 rounds.

Change to 3mm dpns and knit the colourwork pattern following chart B, rounds 1–13 (repeat stitches 1–16, 4 times per round).

Knit 2 rounds with colour 1.

Change to 2.5mm dpns and colour 2: knit 1 round.

*Fourth week of Advent*

Work in k2, p2 rib for 10cm (4in).

Cast off in rib, cut the yarn and weave in loose ends.

Knit one more sock the same way.

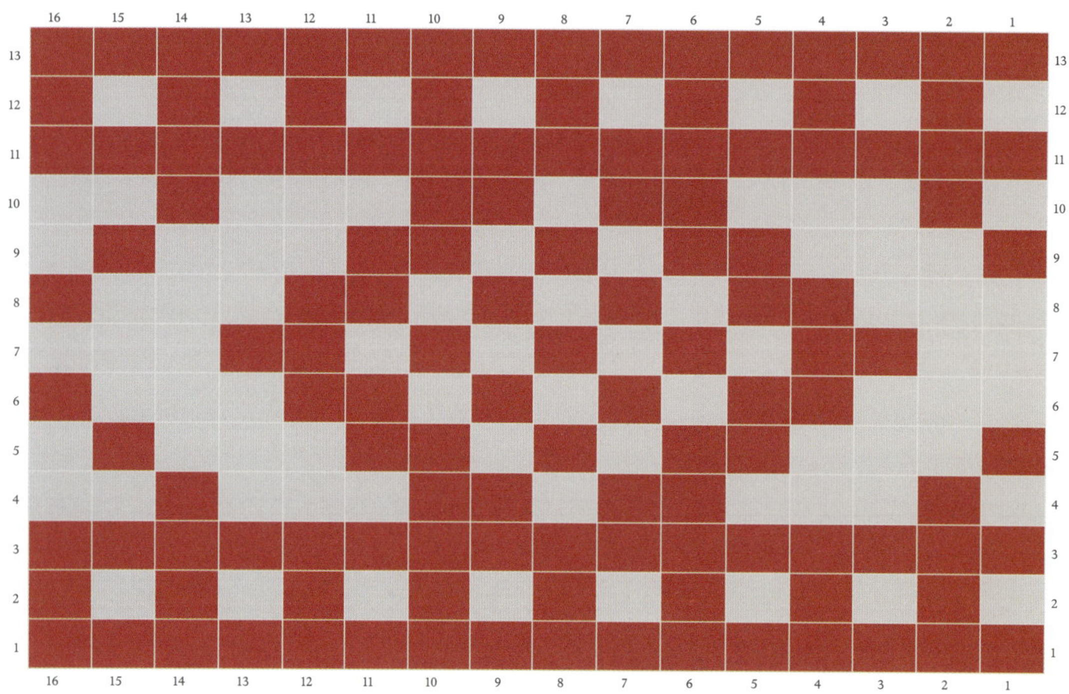

CHART B

# Arctic

The Arctic is a large ocean area by the earth's north pole. It comprises among other things the Arctic Ocean, Greenland, Iceland and the northern parts of Sweden, Norway, Finland, Canada and Russia.

No trees grow in the northernmost part, but mosses, lichens and herbs do. The fauna is made up of herbivores such as reindeer, muskoxen, Arctic hares and lemmings, as well as predators such as snowy owls, Arctic foxes, bears, wolverines, wolves and polar bears.

The name Arctic originates from the Greek word arktos, which means bear. The name refers to the star constellations Ursa Minor (little bear) and Ursa Major (great bear) which are often visible from the northern hemisphere.

Here, Arctic is a collection of three patterns that are primarily designed for those of you who are new to knitting.

The patterns are also suitable for more experienced knitters who want a quick project to knit over a weekend. In the collection are legwarmers, a neckwarmer and a hat. All three garments are knitted in rib.

max ernst
ROUAULT
EHRENSTRAHL

# Legwarmers

YARN: Børstet Alpakka from Sandnes, 96% brushed alpaca, 4% nylon, 50g (1.8oz) = 110m (120yd)

TENSION: 16 sts × 23 rows in stocking stitch using 4.5mm needles = 10 × 10cm (4 × 4in)

SIZE: One size

LEGWARMERS LENGTH: 50cm (19 ¾in)

LEGWARMERS CIRCUMFERENCE:

24–26cm (9 ½–10 ¼in) unstretched

34–36cm (13 ½–14 ¼in) when stretched

AMOUNTS: 150g (5.3oz) Natur Tweed (no. 2523)

DPNS OR CIRCULAR NEEDLE: 3.5mm and 4.5mm

DIFFICULTY LEVEL: 1 of 3

CONSTRUCTION: The legwarmers are knit from the bottom up in rib and are shaped by changing needle size as you go along.

With 3.5mm dpns, cast on 56 sts and divide the stitches evenly over four needles (14 on each needle).

Work in the round in k2, p2 rib until the work measures 20cm (7¾in).

Change to 4.5mm dpns and continue to work in rib until the work measures 40cm (15¾in).

Change back to 3.5mm dpns. Work in rib until the work measures 50cm (19¾in)

Cast off in rib and weave in loose ends. Knit one more legwarmer the same way.

Block the legwarmers carefully following the instructions in the Knitting School, p156 and let dry flat.

# Neckwarmer

YARN: Børstet Alpakka from Sandnes, 96% brushed alpaca, 4% nylon, 50g (1.8oz) = 110m (120yd)

TENSION: 16 sts × 23 rows in stocking stitch using 4.5mm needles = 10 × 10cm (4 × 4in)

SIZE: One size

NECKWARMER LENGTH: 58cm (22 ¾in), with collar folded

NECKWARMER WIDTH: 20cm (7 ¾in)

AMOUNTS: 200g (7.1oz) Natur Tweed (no. 2523)

CIRCULAR NEEDLE: 3.5mm, 40cm (16in) long, and 4.5mm, 60cm (24in) long

NOTIONS: 4 open stitch markers

DIFFICULTY LEVEL: 1 of 3

CONSTRUCTION: The neckwarmer is knit from the top down in rib, and is shaped by increases in the rib. Front and back are worked separately once the shoulder sections are finished.

TECHNIQUES: PM = place marker, see Knitting School, p158.

SM = slip marker, see Knitting School, p158.

M1L = increase 1 st slanting left, see Knitting School, p159.

M1R = increase 1 st slanting right, see Knitting School, p159.

With 3.5mm circular needle, cast on 88 sts. PM at the beginning of the round and work in the round in k2, p2 rib stitch. Repeat until the work measures 20cm (7 ¾in). Change to 4.5mm circular needle.

INCREASE ROUND 1: work (k2, p2) 4 times, k2, PM (see Techniques) , M1L (see Techniques), (p2, k2) 6 times, p2, M1R (see Techniques), PM, (k2, p2) 4 times, k2, PM, M1L, (p2, k2) 6 times, p2,

M1R, SM (the marker at the beginning /end of the round) = 92 sts.

You will now have 4 markers placed for shoulders and for front and back.

INCREASE ROUND 2: Knit the shoulder's rib pattern to M1, SM, M1L. (NB: all increase stitches are knitted in the rib pattern as you go.) Work in rib pattern to M2, M1R, SM. Work the second shoulder's rib pattern to M3, SM, M1L. Work in rib pattern to stitch marker M4 at the beginning/end of the round, M1R, SM = 96 sts.

The 18 rib stitches between M4 and M1 as well as M2 and M3 are the shoulder sections of the neckwarmer.

Repeat increase round 2 a total of 14 times = 152 sts.

Work 1 round in established rib pattern.

## DIVIDE FOR FRONT AND BACK

*Front*

Cut the yarn and place the row's 2 first stitches on a stitch holder. Cast off the following 14 stitches in rib (= right shoulder's stitches), work in rib to the first marker, remove marker. Work in rib to the second marker, remove marker, k2. Turn.

With yarn in front of the work: slip the first stitch purlwise after the turning. Work 61 sts in established rib.

NB: going forward, the neckwarmer's front is worked back and forth in rib. The first stitch on the right side is always slipped knitwise with the yarn at back of the work and the first stitch on the wrong side is always slipped purlwise with the yarn in front of the work.

The remaining stitches from the row can stay on the circular needle, or can be placed on a stitch holder or length of scrap yarn, while the front is knitted.

Work in rib until the front measures 35cm (13 ¾in) from the division, ending with a WS row. Cast off in rib. Cut the yarn.

*Back*

Cast off the remaining 14 stitches for the left shoulder, work in rib to the third marker, remove marker. Work in rib to the fourth marker, remove marker, k2 from the stitch holder, turn and slip the first stitch following previous instructions, work 61 sts in established rib.

Now work the back in rib back and forth until it measures 40cm (15 ¾in) from the division.

Ending with a WS row. Cast off in rib. Cut the yarn and weave in loose ends.

Block the neckwarmer carefully following instructions in the Knitting School, p156 and let dry flat.

POLAROMRÅDENA SYDPOLARLÄNDERNA
NORDPOLARLÄNDERNA
STILLA OCEANEN
NORRA ISHAVET
ÖST-ANTARKTIEN
Rosshavet

# Hat

YARN: Børstet Alpakka from Sandnes, 96% brushed alpaca, 4% nylon, 50g (1.8oz) = 110m (120yd)
TENSION: 16 sts × 23 rows in stocking stitch using 4.5mm needles = 10 × 10cm (4 ×4in)
SIZE: S/M, (L)
HAT CIRCUMFERENCE: 55 (60)cm / 21 ¾ (23 ½)in
HAT LENGTH: 25 (28)cm / 9 ¾ (11)in without fold
AMOUNTS: 50g (100g) / 1.8oz (3.5oz) Natur Tweed (no. 2523)
CIRCULAR NEEDLES: 4.5mm, 40cm (16in) long
NOTIONS: 1 stitch marker
DIFFICULTY LEVEL: 1 of 3
CONSTRUCTION: The hat is knit in the round in rib with decreases at the top.

With 4.5mm circular needle, cast on 72 (80) sts and place a marker on the needle to mark the beginning of the round.
Work in the round in k2, p2 rib stitch until the hat measures 21cm (23cm) / 8 ¼in (9in).

*Decrease for the top of the hat*
ROUND 1: K2, p1, k2tog, *k1, p1, k2tog*, repeat from *–* to last 3 sts, k1, p2tog = 54 (60) sts.
ROUND 2: *K2, p1*, repeat from *–* to end of round.
ROUNDS 3–5: As round 2.
ROUND 6: *K2tog, p1*, repeat from *–* to end of round = 36 (40) sts.
ROUND 7: *K1, p1*, repeat from *–* to end of round.
ROUNDS 8–10: As round 7.
ROUND 11: *K2tog*, repeat from *–* to end of round = 18 (20) sts.
ROUNDS 12–13: Knit.
ROUND 14: *K2tog*, repeat from *–* to end of round = 9 (10) sts.
ROUND 15: Knit.

*Finishing*
Cut the yarn. Pass the yarn through the remaining stitches and weave in. Block the hat carefully following instructions in the Knitting School, p156 and let dry flat.

# Lucia

St. Lucia is celebrated with processions on the 13th of December, led by someone dressed as the saint. In the early 1900s, my great grandma and namesake, Maja, had the role of Lucia in the little Värlmand village, Apertin. I have often admired the old black and white photograph where she stands all dressed in white, with candles in her long, beautiful hair.

The Lucia day tradition is close to my heart. I have celebrated Lucia since childhood and in later years I have had the fortune to see my own daughter be involved in the Lucia processions. The Lucia cardigan is designed to give warmth to the queen of light and is knitted with a combination of two different yarns. It is a feather light cardigan that is suitable for both everyday wear and special occasions.

YARN: Plötulopi from Ístex, 100% Icelandic wool, 100g (3.5oz) = 300m (328yd) and Fin Mohair Silke from Järbo, 72% mohair, 28% silk, 25g (0.9oz) = 210m (230yd)

TENSION: 20 sts × 27 rows in stocking stitch using 4mm needles = 10 × 10cm (4 × 4in)

SIZES: XS (S) M (L) XL (2XL) 3XL

CARDIGAN CHEST WIDTH: 92 (96) 100 (106) 114 (122) 132cm / 36 ¼ (37 ¾) 39 ¼ (41 ¾) 45 (48) 52in

CARDIGAN LENGTH: 48 (50) 50 (53) 54 (57) 57cm / 19 (19 ¾) 19 ¾ (20 ¾) 22 ½ (22 ½) 22 ½in

SLEEVE LENGTH: 43 (43) 44 (44) 46 (46) 46cm / 17 (17) 17 ¼ (17 ¼) 18 (18) 18in

AMOUNTS: Colour 1 Plötulopi = 300 (300) 300 (400) 400 (450) 500 g / 10.6 (10.6) 10.6 (14.1) 14.1 (15.9) 17.6oz (no. 1026, Light Ash Heather), colour 2 Fin Mohair Silke = 125 (125) 125 (150) 150 (175) 200 g /4.4 (4.4) 4.4 (5.3) 5.3 (6.2) 7.1oz (no. 31531, Arctic Wolf)

CIRCULAR NEEDLES: 3.5mm and 4mm, 80cm (32in) long

DOUBLE-POINTED NEEDLES: 3.5mm and 4mm

NOTIONS: Stitch markers

DIFFICULTY LEVEL: 3 of 3

CONSTRUCTION: The cardigan is knit with two different yarns held together. It is knit back and forth, from the top and down in one piece, with raglan increases and decreases at the sides. To finish, button band and neckband are knit on.

TECHNIQUES: PM = place marker, see Knitting School, p158.
SM = slip marker, see Knitting School, p158.
Kfb = knit in the front loop and back loop of the same stitch.
M1L = increase 1 st slanting left, see Knitting School, p159.
M1R = increase 1 st slanting right, see Knitting School, p159.

## YOKE

With 4mm circular needle and one strand of each yarn, cast on 76 (76) 80 (80) 84 (88) 90 sts.

FIRST ROW (WS): P2 (= right front), PM (see Techniques), p20 (= right sleeve), PM, p32 (32) 36 (36) 40 (44) 46 (= back), PM, p20 (= left sleeve), PM, p2 (= left front).

RAGLAN INCREASES, INCREASE ROW 1 (RS): K1, KFB (see Techniques), SM (see Abbreviations), KFB. Knit to last st before next marker, KFB, SM, KFB. Knit to last st before next marker, KFB, SM, KFB. Knit to last st before next marker, KFB, SM, KFB, k1 = 8 sts increased = 84 (84) 88 (88) 92 (96) 98 sts.

ROW 2: Purl.

ROW 3: K1, M1L (see Techniques), (knit to last st before next marker, KFB, SM, KFB) 4 times. Knit to last st before end of row, M1R (see Techniques), k1 = 10 sts increased = 94 (94) 98 (98) 102 (106) 108 sts.

ROW 4: Purl.

ROWS 5–16: Repeat rows 3 and 4 another 6 times = 154 (154) 158 (158) 162 (166) 168 sts.

ROW 17: (Knit to last st before next marker, KFB, SM, KFB) 4 times. Knit to end of row, don't turn, instead cast on 5 (5) 7 (7) 9 (11) 12 sts using the double twisted loop technique (see Video links in the Knitting School, p160), turn.

ROW 18: Purl to end of row, don't turn, instead cast on 5 (5) 7 (7) 9 (11) 12 sts using the double twisted loop technique = 172 (172) 180 (180) 188 (196) 200 sts, of which 23 (23) 25 (25) 27 (29) 30 sts = fronts, 38 sts = sleeves, 50 (50) 54 (54) 58 (62) 64 sts = back.

Continue to raglan increases as follows.

### A

ROW 1 (INCREASE 8 STS, RS): (Knit to last st before next marker, KFB, SM, KFB) 4 times, knit to end of row = 180 (180) 188 (188) 196 (204) 208 sts.

ROW 2: Purl.

Repeat rows 1 and 2 another 1 (2) 3 (3) 7 (9) 11 times = 188 (196) 212 (212) 252 (276) 296 sts.

### B

ROW 1 (INCREASE 4 STS, RS): (Knit to last st before next marker, KFB, SM, knit to next marker, SM, KFB) 2 times, knit to end of row = 192 (200) 216 (216) 256 (280) 300 sts.

ROW 2: Purl.

ROW 3 (INCREASE 8 STS, RS): (Knit to last st before next marker, KFB, SM, KFB) 4 times, knit to end of row = 200 (208) 224 (224) 264 (288) 308 sts.

ROW 4: Purl.

Repeat rows 1–4 another 2 (2) 1 (3) 1 (1) 1 times = 224 (232) 236 (260) 276 (300) 320 sts.

Repeat rows 1 and 2 another 5 (6) 5 (5) 6 (6) 7 times = 244 (256) 256 (280) 300 (324) 348 sts.

### C

*XS, S, M, L and XL*

ROW 1: Knit.

ROW 2: Purl.

ROW 3 (INCREASE 4 STS, RS): *Knit to last st before marker, KFB, SM, knit to next marker, SM, KFB*, repeat from *–* once more, knit to end of row = 248 (260) 260 (284) 304 (328) 352 sts.

ROW 4: Purl.

Repeat rows 1–4 another 1 (1) 2 (1) 1 (0) 0 times = 252 (264) 268 (288) 308 (328) 352 sts.

*All sizes, XS–3XL*

Work 2 (2) 2 (2) 2 (4) 2 rows in stocking stitch (= knit on the right side and purl on the wrong side).

*Divide for body and sleeves*

*Knit to next marker, remove the marker, place the following 48 (50) 50 (54) 58 (62) 66 sts onto a stitch holder or a length of scrap yarn, remove marker. Cast on 6 (6) 7 (7) 8 (9) 10 sts using the double twisted loop technique, PM, cast on 6 (6) 7 (7) 8 (9) 10 sts using the double twisted loop technique *, repeat from *–* once more, knit to end of row = 180 (188) 196 (208) 224 (240) 260 sts, of which 44 (46) 48 (51) 55 (59) 64 sts = fronts, 92 (96) 100 (106) 114 (122) 132 sts = back.

## BODY

Work in stocking stitch until the body measures 5cm (2in) from the armhole, finishing with a wrong side row.

DECREASE ROW: *Knit to last 3 sts before marker, k2tog, k1, SM, k1, SL1, k1 and pass the slipped st over the one you've just knitted*, repeat from *–* once more, knit to end of row = 176 (184) 192 (204) 220 (236) 256 sts.

*Continue in stocking stitch for 7cm (2 ¾in), finishing with a wrong side row. Work the decrease row as above* = 172 (180) 188 (200) 216 (232) 252 sts, repeat from *–* once more = 168 (176) 184 (196) 212 (228) 248 sts.

Continue working in stocking stitch until the work measures 20 (20) 20 (22) 22 (24) 24cm / 7 ¾ (7 ¾) 7 ¾ (8 ¾) 8 ¾ (9 ½) 9 ½in from the armhole. Finish with a wrong side row.

Knit one row and at the same time decrease 1 st = 167 (175) 183 (195) 211 (227) 247 sts.

Purl 1 row.

## RIB CUFF

Change to 3.5mm circular needle.

ROW 1: K1, *p1, k1*, repeat from *–* to end of row.

ROW 2: P1, *k1, p1*, repeat from *–* to end of row.

Repeat rows 1 and 2 until the rib measures 5cm (2in). Finish with a wrong side row.

Cast off in rib.

## SLEEVES

With 4mm dpns: Starting at the bottom of the armhole, pick up 6 (6) 7 (7) 8 (9) 10 sts.

Place the 48 (50) 50 (54) 58 (62) 66 sleeve stitches on the needle, pick up 6 (6) 7 (7) 8 (9) 10 sts under the armhole, PM = 60 (62) 64 (68) 74 (80) 86 sts.

Knit in the round in stocking stitch (= knit every row when knitting in the round) for 6 rounds.

DECREASE ROUND: K1, k2tog, knit to last 3 sts of the round, SL1, k1 and pass the slipped st over the one you've just knitted, k1 = 58 (60) 62 (66) 72 (78) 84 sts.

XS: Continue decrease every 4cm (1 ½in) another 2 times = 54 sts. Then decrease every 3cm (1 ¼in) another 7 times = 40 sts. Knit 4 rounds.

S: Continue decrease every 3cm (1 ¼in) another 8 times = 44 sts. Then decrease every 2cm (¾in) another 2 times = 40 sts. Knit 4 rounds.

M: Continue decrease every 3cm (1 ¼in) another 9 times = 44 sts. Then decrease every 2cm (¾in) once more = 42 sts. Knit 4 rounds.

L: Continue decrease every 3cm (1 ¼in) another 5 times = 56 sts. Then decrease every 2cm (¾in) another 6 times = 44 sts. Knit 4 rounds.

XL: Continue decrease every 3cm (1 ¼in) another 3 times = 66 sts. Then decrease every 2cm (¾in) another 9 times = 48 sts. Knit 4 rounds.

2XL: Continue decrease every 3cm (1 ¼in) another 5 times = 68 sts. Then decrease every 2cm (¾in) round another 10 times = 48 sts. Knit 6 rounds.

3XL: Continue decrease every 2cm (¾in) another 17 times = 50 sts. Knit 4 rounds.

Continue working in stocking stitch until the sleeve measures 39 (39) 40 (40) 42 (42) 42cm / 15 ½ (15 ½) 15 ¾ (15 ¾) 16 ½ (16 ½) 16 ½in from the armhole.

Change to 3.5mm dpns and work in k1, p1 rib until the rib cuff measures 4cm (1 ½in).

Cast off in rib.

## BUTTON BANDS

*Left button band*

With 3.5mm circular needle and the right side facing you, pick up stitches along the left starting at the top. To make the edge stretchy enough, pick up 7 of 8 sts (= *pick up 7 st, skip the 8th st*, repeat from *–*). The final number of stitches should be odd.

Work in rib (WS): P2, *k1, p1*, repeat from *–* to last st of the row, p1. Continue working in established rib for a total of 9 rows. Then cast off in rib.

*Right button band*

Mark the placement of the buttonholes by placing safety pins in the left button band. The bottom buttonhole should be placed 2cm (¾in) from the edge. The top buttonhole should be placed in the middle of the neckband and will therefore be placed 2cm (¾in) above the button band. Between these you divide 3 buttonholes evenly.

With 3.5mm circular needle and right side facing you, pick up stitches along the right side starting from the bottom, the same way as for the left button band. Make sure that you get the same number of stitches!

WORK IN RIB (WS): P2, *k1, p1*, repeat from *–* to last st on the row, p1. Continue working in established rib for a total of 5 rows.

BUTTONHOLE ROW: *Work in established rib to the buttonhole marker. (NB: the buttonhole goes over 2 sts.) K2tog, yo*. Repeat from *–* until 5 buttonholes have been worked, work in rib to end of row.

Work in rib another 3 rows. Cast off in rib.

## NECKBAND

With 3.5mm circular needle and right side facing you, pick up stitches for the neckband, 8 sts along the button band, 15 (15) 17 (17) 19 (21) 22 sts along the right front, 20 sts along the right sleeve, 31 (31) 35 (35) 35 (35) 39 sts along the back, 20 sts along the left sleeve, 15 (15) 17 (17) 19 (21) 22 sts along the left front, 8 sts along the button band = 117 (117) 125 (125) 129 (133) 139 sts.

ROW 1 (WS): P1, *k1, p1*, repeat from *–* to end of row.

ROW 2 (RS): K1, *p1, k1* repeat from *–* to end of row.

Work in established rib for another 7 rows. NB: on row 6 a buttonhole is knitted as follows: K1, p1 k1, k2tog, yo. Then continue working in established rib to end of row.

Cast off in rib.

## FINISHING

Weave in loose ends. Sew on buttons level with the buttonholes.

Block the cardigan carefully to given measurements and following instructions in the Knitting School p156.

# Christmas tree

My Christmas tree is decorated with glistening, old Christmas tree baubles made from glass – you know those that are so delicate that you barely dare to touch them? Straw decorations and various other kinds of inherited decorations also dangle there: christmas wreaths hungwith paper angel book marks, plastic baubles from the 1960s with a Santa orchestra and colourful crackers. On the tree is also a shiny Christmas apple that I got from my teacher in first class, a glass prism in the shape of a star that was a Christmas present from my parents and two small Christmas tree Santas made of yarn, that sit furthest in by the trunk and watch over Christmas.

The Christmas tree socks are a tribute to all the Christmas trees in my life – from tabletop trees to plastic trees.

YARN: Järbo Mellanraggi, 75% wool superwash, 25% polyamide, 100g = 260m (284yd)

TENSION: 30 sts × 42 rows in stocking stitch in pattern with 2.5mm needles = 10 × 10 cm (4 × 4in)

SIZES: UK 1/2 (3/4) 5/6 (7/8) / EU 34/35 (36/37) 38/39 (40/41)

SOCK CIRCUMFERENCE: 16 (18) 19 (20)cm / 6 ¼ (7) 7 ½ (7 ¾)in

SOCK LENGTH: 22 (23) 24 (25)cm / 8 ¾ (9) 9 ½ (9 ¾)in

LEG CIRCUMFERENCE: 16 (18) 19 (20)cm / 6 ¼ (7) 7 ½ (7 ¾)in

LEG LENGTH: 19cm (7 ½in)

AMOUNTS: Colour 1 = 150 (200) 200 (200)g / 5.3 (7.1) 7.1 (7.1)oz Light Grey (no. 28211), colour 2 = 50 (50) 50 (50)g / 1.8 (1.8) 1.8 (1.8) oz Forest Green (no. 28237)

DOUBLE-POINTED NEEDLES: 2.5mm

NOTIONS: 4 stitch markers

DIFFICULTY LEVEL: 2 of 3

CONSTRUCTION: The socks are knit from the leg down with rib, colourwork leg and fleegle heel.

TECHNIQUES: M1L = increase 1 st slanting left, see Knitting School, p159.

M1R = increase 1 st slanting right, see Knitting School, p159.

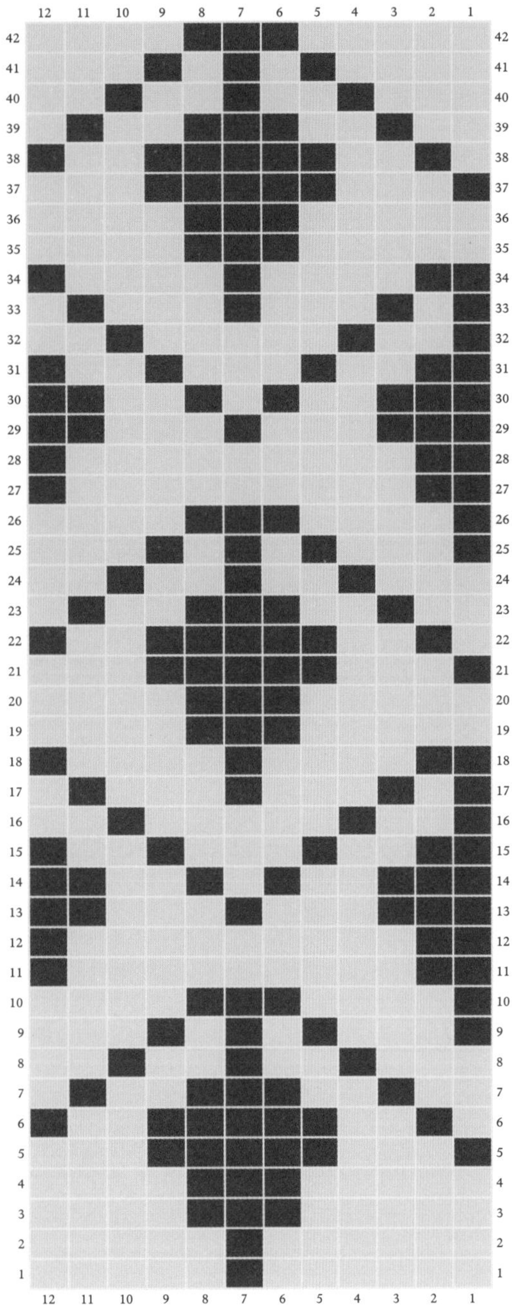

## LEG

With 2.5mm dpns and colour 1, cast on 72 sts and divide the stitches evenly over four needles.

Work in the round in k2, p2 rib stitch for 4cm (1 ½in).

Now work in stocking stitch (= knit all stitches when working in the round) and knit 2 rounds. Knit colourwork pattern following the chart, rounds 1–42 (stitches 1–12 are repeated across the whole round).

With colour 1: Knit 2 rounds.

Work in k2, p2 rib for 2.5cm (1in). Continue working in stocking stitch. Knit 1 round.

Decrease 24 (20) 16 (12) sts evenly spaced over the round = 48 (52) 56 (60) sts.

## HEEL GUSSET

Stitches 1–24 (1–26) 1–28 (1–30) = top. Stitches 25–48 (27–52) 29–56 (31–60) = bottom. Continue to work in the round but increase at each side of the sock's bottom following instructions for round 1.

ROUND 1: Top: Knit all stitches. Bottom: K1, M1L (see Techniques), knit to last st, M1R (see Techniques), k1.

ROUND 2: Knit.

Repeat rounds 1 and 2 until you have 46 (50) 54 (58) sts at the bottom. NB: finish with round 2.

## HEEL

Knit the stiches on the top in stocking stitch. Then place a marker in the middle of the two middle stitches at the bottom.

Now the bottom is knitted back and forth in stocking stitch with decreases at the sides for the following rows.

ROW 1 (RS): Knit to marker, k2, k2tog, k1, turn.

ROW 2 (WS): SL1 purlwise, hold yarn taut, and purl to marker, p2, ssp tbl (= slip the next 2 sts knitwise, one at a time, from the left needle to the right, then transfer them back to the left needle [they are now twisted] and then purl together through the back loop), p1, turn.

ROW 3 (RS): SL1 and hold yarn taut, knit to last st before the gap created by the previous turning. Knit together the stitches before and after the gap (= k2tog), k1, turn.

ROW 4 (WS): SL1 purlwise and hold yarn taut, purl to last st before the gap, work together the stitches before and after the gap (= ssp tbl), p1, turn.

Repeat rows 3 and 4 until 2 unworked stitches remain after a wrong side row. Turn.

NEXT ROW (RS): As row 3 but don't turn, instead continue across the top.

NEXT ROW: Top: Knit. Bottom: k1, k2tog tbl (= k2tog through the back loop), knit to last 3 sts, k2tog, k1.

NEXT ROW: Top: Knit. Bottom: k1, k2tog tbl, knit the remaining stitches. Now you will once again have 24 (26) 28 (30) sts at the bottom, 48 (52) 56 (60) sts in total.

## FOOT

Work in stocking stitch until the foot measures 16.5 (17.5) 18.5 (19.5)cm / 6 ½ (6 ¾) 7 ¼ (7 ¾)in

## TOE

DECREASE ROUND: K1, SL1, k1 and pass the slipped st over the one you've just knitted, knit to last 3 sts on needle 2, k2tog, k1. Needle 3: K1, SL1, k1 and pass the slipped st over the one you've just knitted, knit to last 3 sts on needle 4, k2tog, k1 = 4 sts decreased on the round.

Repeat the decreases every other round until 16 (20) 20 (24) sts remain on the needles.

Cast off using the 3-needle cast off technique, see Knitting School, p160.

Knit one more sock the same way.

# Fura

I often take inspiration from the conifer trees' beautiful branches for my knit designs. When the pine (*Pinus sylvestris*) grows really old is called fura in Swedish. Did you know that the pine needles are really a kind of rolled up leaf that is coated in wax to make it withstand the winter? The needles contain both vitamin C and sugar, which means that pine needles can give us Northerners vital energy during winter. You can boil together a vitamin-rich drink from a couple of handfuls of pine needles and 500ml of water.

The Fura half mittens are soft, warm and adorned with a stylised two-colour pattern. They sit extra snug on the hands thanks to the ribbed thumb.

YARN: Fivel from Rauma Garn, 100% Norwegian lamb's wool, 50g (1.8oz) = 100m (109yd)

TENSION: 21 sts × 24 rows stocking stitch in pattern with 4mm needles = 10 × 10cm (4 × 4in)

SIZES: One size

MITTEN LENGTH: 21cm (8 ¼in)

MITTEN WIDTH: 9.5cm (3 ¾in)

AMOUNTS: Colour 1 = 50g (1.8oz) Mørk grønn (no. 24), colour 2 = 50g (1.8oz) Mintgrønn melert (no. 301)

DOUBLE-POINTED NEEDLES: 4mm

DIFFICULTY LEVEL: 2 of 3

CONSTRUCTION: The half mitten is knit in the round in one piece with a ribbed afterthought thumb.

## RIGHT MITTEN

With 4mm dpns and colour 1, cast on 40 sts and divide them evenly over four needles (10 sts on each needle). Work in the round in k2, p2 rib for 5cm (2in).

Change to stocking stitch (= knit all stitches when working in the round).

Knit following the chart, rounds 1–24 (stitches 1–40).

### *Prepare for thumb*

Change to colour 1 and knit the round's first 20 sts. Then take a loose end of yarn in a contrasting colour and knit the following 8 sts with it. Transfer these 8 sts to the left needle and knit them with colour 1. Knit the remaining 12 sts.

### *Continue the hand*

Work in k2, p2 rib for 5cm (2in). Cast off in rib. Weave in loose ends.

### *Thumb*

Remove the yarn that marks the thumb.

With four dpns and colour 1, pick up the 16 thumb stitches and work in the round in k2, p2 rib stitch until the thumb measures 3cm (1 ¼in). Cast off in rib. Weave in loose ends.

## LEFT MITTEN

Knit as for right half mitten, but mirror the chart by following it from left to right instead of right to left.

Knit the yarn that marks the thumb on the round's 8 last stitches (stitches 33–40).

# Winter rose

Winter rose or Christmas rose is what we call hellebore in Swedish. It comes from southeast Europe and on our latitude it can start flowering as early as December, if the winter is mild. The flower was spread across Europe in medieval times by monks. In folklore, a hellebore was said to protect against evil spirits, witches and other creatures.

The Winter rose cardigan will light up your winter darkness! Choose colours according to your mood. Perhaps you want to capture the hellebore's white petals or, like me, embrace your love for pink? The main thing is that you find colours that make you happy.

YARN: Järbo 2 tr ull, 100% wool, 100g (3.5oz) = 300m (328yd)

TENSION: 25 sts × 30 rows in stocking stitch in pattern with 3mm needles = 10 × 10cm (4 × 4in)

SIZES: XS (S) M (L) XL (2XL) 3XL

CARDIGAN CHEST WIDTH: 87 (96) 105 (115) 125 (134) 143cm / 34 ¼ (37 ¾) 41 ¼ (45 ¼) 49 ¼ (52 ¾) 56 ¼in

CARDIGAN LENGTH: 42 (43) 45 (46) 48 (51) 53cm / 16 ½ (17) 17 ¾ (18) 19 (20) 20 ¾in

SLEEVE LENGTH: 48 (49) 50 (50) 50 (53) 53cm / 19 (19 ¼) 19 ¾ (19 ¾) 19 ¾ (20 ¾) 20 ¾in

AMOUNTS: Colour 1 = 100 (100) 100 (100) 100 (100) 100g / 3.5oz, Ash (no. 74108), colour 2 = 300 (300) 300 (400) 450 (450) 500g / 10.6 (10.6) 10.6 (14.1) 15.9 (15.9) 17.6oz, Silver Stream (no. 74104), colour 3 = 150 (150) 150 (150) 150 (150) (150)g / 5.3oz, Pink Pop (no. 74127), colour 4 = 150 (150) 150 (150) 150 (150) 150g / 5.3oz, Tree Hugger (no. 74149)

CIRCULAR NEEDLES: 2.5mm and 3mm, 80cm (32in) long

DOUBLE-POINTED NEEDLES: 2.5mm and 3mm

NOTIONS: 5 stitch markers, stitch holder, 11 buttons (10mm in diameter), decorative band (optional)

DIFFICULTY LEVEL: 3 of 3

CONSTRUCTION: The cardigan is knit in the round from the bottom up, body and sleeves worked separately. The parts are then knit together for the yoke. To finish, button bands are knit on and the cardigan is cut open (see Knitting School, p154).

TECHNIQUES: M1L = increase 1 st slanting left, see Knitting School, p159.

M1R = increase 1 st slanting right, see Knitting School, p159.

Raglan decreases = knit to last 3 sts before raglan marker, SL1, k1 and pass the slipped st over the one you've just knitted, k1, slip marker from left to right needle, k1, k2tog. Repeat at all raglan markers.

## BODY

With 2.5mm circular needle and colour 1, cast on 218 (242) 266 (290) 314 (338) 362 sts. Work in rib back and forth.

ROW 1 (WS): *P2, k2*, repeat from *–* to last 2 sts, p2.

ROW 2 (RS): *K2, p2*, repeat from *–* to last 2 sts, k2.

ROW 3 (WS): *P2, k2*, repeat from *–* to last 2 sts, p2. Repeat rows 2 and 3 until the rib measures 5cm (2in). NB: finish the rib with a wrong side row.

Change to 3mm circular needle. Knit to end of row and at the same time decrease 1 (1) 1 (1) 1 (1) 1 st = 217 (241) 265 (289) 313 (337) 361 sts. Then cast on 5 steek stitches using the double twisted loop technique (see video links in the Knitting School on p160).

The steek stitches also function as a marker for the beginning and end of a row. (NB: the steek stitches are not included in the cardigan's total stitch count and increases and decreases should not be made within these stitches.) Going forward the body is knitted in the round in stocking stich (= knit every round when knitting in the round).

Knit the pattern following the chart, rounds 1–8 (stitches 1–6 are repeated to last st on the round, then stitch 1 on the chart is knitted) Then repeat rounds 9–16 until the work measures 26 (26) 27 (28) 30 (32) 34cm / 10 ¼ (10 ¼) 10 ½ (11) 11 ¾ (12 ½) 13 ½in or length of your choice. NB: finish with round 12 or 16 in the chart.

Cast off as follows: Knit 50 (55) 60 (65) 70 (75) 80 sts, cast off 9 (11) 13 (15) 17 (19) 21 st (after casting off 1 st remains on the right needle). Knit 98 (108) 118 (128) 138 (148) 158 sts, cast off 9 (11) 13 (15) 17 (19) 21 sts (after casting off 1 st remains on the right needle), knit 49 (54) 59 (64) 69 (74) 79 sts = 198 (218) 238 (258) 278 (298) 318 st. Transfer the stitches for the body onto a stitch holder/length of scrap yarn and set the work aside.

## RIGHT SLEEVE

With 2.5mm dpns and colour 1, cast on 60 (60) 60 (60) 64 (64) 64 sts.

Work in the round in k2, p2 rib stitch for 5cm (2in).

Going forward the sleeve is knitted in stocking stitch. Change to 3mm dpns, knit 1 round and at the same time increase 0 (0) 0 (0) 8 (8) 8 sts evenly spaced over the round = 60 (60) 60 (60) 72 (72) 72 sts.

Knit pattern following the chart, rounds 1–16 (repeat stitches 1–6 to end of round). NB: place a stitch marker on the needle at the beginning of the round – to make it easier to ensure the pattern is evenly placed.

Now increases are started at the same time as repeating rounds 9–16 of the chart. New stitches are incorporated into the established pattern.

INCREASE ROUND: K1, M1L (see Techniques), knit to last st on the round, M1R (see Techniques), k1. Continue to work in pattern in stocking stitch and repeat the increase round every 2.5 (2.5) 2.5 (2) 2 (2) 2cm /1 (1) 1 (¾) ¾ (¾) ¾in gap, to last 82 (86) 90 (96) 100 (106) 110 sts on the needle. Work until the sleeve measures approximately 48 (49) 50 (50) 50 (53) 53cm / 19 (19 ¼) 19 ¾ (19 ¾) 19 ¾ (20 ¾) 20 ¾in, but adjust the length according to the colourwork pattern. NB: finish with round 11 or 15 in the chart so that the following round becomes the same final round as you made for the body (= round 12 or round 16 in the chart).

Finish by casting off at the middle bottom of the sleeve as follows: cast off 4 (5) 6 (7) 8 (9) 10 sts, knit to last 5 (6) 7 (8) 9 (10) 11 sts on the round, cast off 5 (6) 7 (8) 9 (10) 11 sts = 73 (75) 77 (81) 83 (87) 89 sts. Transfer the stitches for the sleeve onto a stitch holder or a length of scrap yarn and set the work aside.

Adjusting the length of the cardigan: the Winter rose cardigan is waist length. If you wish to make a longer cardigan you can lengthen the body by knitting a further 10cm (4in), or number of centimetres of your choice. If you make the cardigan 10cm (4in) longer, you will need 70–100g (2.5oz–3.5oz) extra of colour 2.

## LEFT SLEEVE

Worked as right sleeve, but the pattern chart is mirrored to make the sleeves look the same from the front.

## YOKE

Now all parts are worked together in established pattern. NB: the 4 sts before and after the raglan markers are now worked with colour 2.

With 3mm circular needle and right side facing you. Knit the parts together on the circular needle in the order below. NB: at the same time, place markers as follows:

1 marker at beginning of round, 1 raglan marker in the transition between right front and right sleeve, 1 raglan marker in the transition between right sleeve and back, 1 raglan marker in the transition between back and left sleeve and 1 raglan marker in the transition between left sleeve and left front.

Right front: 50 (55) 60 (65) 70 (75) 80 sts.
Right sleeve: 73 (75) 77 (81) 83 (87) 89 sts.
Back: 99 (109) 119 (129) 139 (149) 159 sts.
Left sleeve: 73 (75) 77 (81) 83 (87) 89 sts.
Left front: 50 (55) 60 (65) 70 (75) 80 sts.
Now you have a total of 345 (369) 393 (421) 445 (473) 497 sts on the needle. Continue knitting colourwork pattern following the chart, with the same placement as before for each part respectively. Let the 'roses' on the different parts gradually phase out as the number of stitches are decreased at the raglan decreases.

Raglan decreases: Work in stocking stitch and make raglan decreases (see Techniques) on each round, a total of 7 (8) 8 (9) 10 (12) 14 times. Then make raglan decreases every other round, a total of 19 (21) 23 (24) 25 (23) 23 times = 137 (137) 145 (157) 165 (193) 201 sts on the needle.

## NECKBAND

Knit to last 10 (10) 10 (11) 11 (12) 12 sts before the steek stitches and then cast off 20 (20) 20 (22) 22 (24) 24 sts plus the 5 steek stitches in the middle – this forms the neckband. Continue to work the row that was started with casting off and make raglan decreases as before for this row.

Going forward the rest of the cardigan is worked back and forth in the pattern. Turn and p2tog, then purl to end of row. Continue working in stocking stitch (= knit on the right side and purl on the wrong side). In addition, decrease 1 st at the beginning of each row as follows (RS): SL1, k1 and pass the slipped st over the one you've just knitted. (WS): P2tog. On the right side, continue with raglan decreases until a total of 24 (26) 28 (29) 30 (30) 31 decreases have been made on every other row. The 7 (8) 8 (9) 10 (12) 14 initial raglan decreases are NOT included in this number. NB: the two final raglan decrease rows are not knit in pattern but solely with colour 1.

After the final row with raglan decreases, work a final wrong side row as follows: P2tog, purl to last 2 sts on the needle, p2tog = 67 (67) 75 (85) 93 (99) 97 sts.

Set these stitches aside.

## BUTTON BANDS

*Right button band (with buttonholes)*

With 3mm circular needle and colour 2 (RS), pick up 116 (116) 118 (120) 124 (128) 132 sts along the right front edge starting from the bottom. NB: distribute the stitches evenly by skipping every fourth row when picking up stitches. (= *pick up 3 sts, skip the fourth st*, repeat from *–*). Knit 3 rows.

Now start the buttonholes: (XS): K2, *k2tog, yo, k9*, repeat from *–* 9 times, k2tog, yo, k2. (S): K2, *k2tog, yo, k9*, repeat from *–* 9 times, k2tog, yo, k2. (M): K3, *k2tog, yo, k9*, repeat from *–* 9 times, k2tog, yo, k3. (L): K4, *k2tog, yo, k9*, repeat from *–* 9 times, k2tog, yo, k4. (XL): K6, *k2tog, yo, k9*. Repeat from *–* 9 times, k2tog, yo, k6. (2XL): K3, *k2tog, yo, k10*, repeat from *–* 9 times, k2tog, yo, k3. 3XL: K5, *k2tog, yo, k10*, repeat from *–* 9 times, k2tog, yo, k5. Knit 3 rows.

To get a sturdy edge that doesn't stretch with use, every fourth stitch is decreased when casting off, as follows: *Cast off 3 sts, k2tog, cast off the stitch that was knitted together*, repeat from *–* until all stitches have been cast off. NB: the cast off might be completed in the middle of a repetition.

*Left button band*

With 3mm circular needle and colour 2 (RS), pick up 116 (116) 118 (120) 124 (128) 132 sts along the left front starting at the top. Knit 7 rows.

Cast off as for the right button band.

## NECKBAND

With right side facing you and starting at the right button band, 3mm circular needle and colour 2: Pick up new stitches along the right neckband – 1 st in each of the following 3 sts, skip 1 st and repeat until you reach the existing stitches. Knit 67 (67) 75 (85) 93 (99) 97 sts and then pick up the same number of stitches along the left neckband as you picked up at the beginning of the row before the existing stitches. Knit 5 rows, back and forth.

Cast off as for right button band.

## CUTTING THE STEEK

See Knitting School, p154. Sew a reinforcing seam with sewing thread (by hand, using backstitch) on each side of the middle steek stitch. Carefully cut the cardigan open in the middle of the middle steek stitch. (The cut edges will roll in towards the wrong side.)

## FINISHING

Sew the body together underneath the armholes using kitchener stitch (see Knitting School, p160). Weave in loose ends.

Block the cardigan carefully following the measurements specified and instructions in the Knitting School, p156.

Sew on buttons level with the buttonholes. Either cover the cut edges on the inside with a decorative band, or fold them in and sew with discreet stitches to the wrong side.

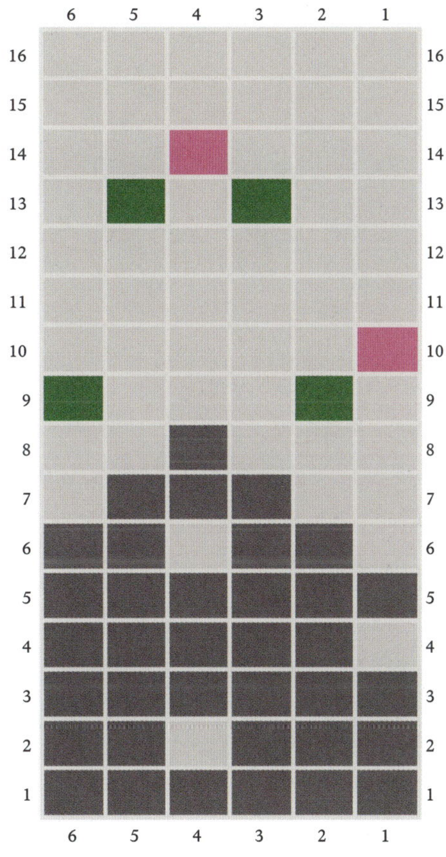

# Christmas Day

Christmas Day is my favourite day over the festive period. Calm, undemanding and filled with all those things that make Christmas. First, Christmas Day service with glistening candles and grand music. It's so beautiful to step right into the light, from the dark winter night.

Then the day continues with walks in the snow – play and games. Sometimes we eat Värmland sausages with mustard sauce for lunch. Perhaps we eat ris à la malta in the evening. Reading a Christmas gift book under a warm blanket, or knitting a few rows on a mitten are other things I like to do on Christmas Day. The Christmas Day collared mittens are lavish and snug, perfect for wearing to Christmas Day service, or winter walks when you want to be extra nice and festive. A collared mitten is a mitten with extra width in the cuff.

YARN: Finullgarn from Rauma Ullvarefabrikk, 100% pure virgin wool, 50g (1.8oz) = 175m (191yd)

TENSION: 29 sts × 30 rows in stocking stitch in pattern with 3mm needles = 10 × 10cm (4 × 4in)

SIZES: One size

MITTEN WIDTH: 9.5cm (3 ¾in)

MITTEN LENGTH: 26cm (10 ¼in)

AMOUNTS: Colour 1 = 100g (3.5oz) Lys beige melert (no. 4078), colour 2 = 30g (1oz) Mosegrønn melert (no. 4129), colour 3 = 50g (1.8oz) Aubergine (no. 441)

DOUBLE-POINTED NEEDLES: 2.5mm and 3mm

DIFFICULTY LEVEL: 3 of 3

CONSTRUCTION: The collared mittens are knit from the cuff up with a traditional afterthought thumb.

TECHNIQUES: Ridges: Created by alternating knit and purl rows on a circular needle.

## RIGHT MITTEN

### *Collar*

With 3mm dpns and colour 1, cast on 72 sts using the liksiding uppläggning technique (see video links in the Knitting School, p160) and divide them evenly over four needles (18 sts on each needle). Working in the round, purl 1 round.

*Knit 1 round, purl 1 round*, repeat from *–* once more. Now a total of 3 ridges have been formed.

Work in stocking stitch for 2 rounds (= knit all stitches when working in the round).

Then knit the colourwork pattern following chart A, rounds 1–9 (stitches 1–6 are repeated to end of round).

Then knit 2 rounds.

DECREASE ROUND: *K4, k2tog*, repeat from *–* to end of round = 60 sts.

### *Rib*

Change to 2.5mm dpns and work in k2, p2 rib for 10 rounds.

### *Hand*

Change to 3mm dpn, work in stocking stitch going forward.

Knit 1 round with colour 1. Knit another round and decrease 4 sts evenly spaced over the round = 56 sts.

Knit colourwork pattern following chart B1, rounds 1–15 (stitches 1–28 are repeated 2 times per round).

### *Prepare for thumb*

Knit colourwork pattern following chart B1 (round 16) for the round's initial 30 sts. Then take a length of yarn in a contrasting colour and knit the following 11 sts with it. Transfer these 11 sts back onto the left needle. Knit the 11 sts again, now with colour 3, and then the rest of the stitches on the round following the chart.

### *Continue the hand*

Knit colourwork pattern according to chart B1, rounds 17–33, and then continue with colour 1 until the hand measures 9cm (3 ½in) from the thumb.

DECREASE ROUND FOR THE TOP OF THE MITTEN:

K1, SL1, k1 and pass the slipped st over the one you've just knit, and knit to last 2 sts on needle 2: K2tog. Needle 3: K1, SL1, k1 and pass the slipped st over the one you've just knit, and knit to last 2 sts on needle 4: K2tog = 4 sts decreased.

Repeat the decrease round twice every other round, and then each round until 8 sts remain. Cut the yarn, pass the thread through the remaining stitches and secure the yarn.

### *Thumb*

Remove the yarn that marks the thumb.

With 3mm dpns, pick up the 22 thumb stitches and knit in the round in pattern following chart B2, rounds 1–3 (stitches 1–11 are repeated twice per round).

With colour 1, continue knitting until the thumb measures 5.5cm (2 ¼in).

Decrease following the same principle as for the top of the mitten, but for each round, until 10 sts remain.

Cut the yarn, pass the thread through the remaining stitches and pull tight. Weave in loose ends.

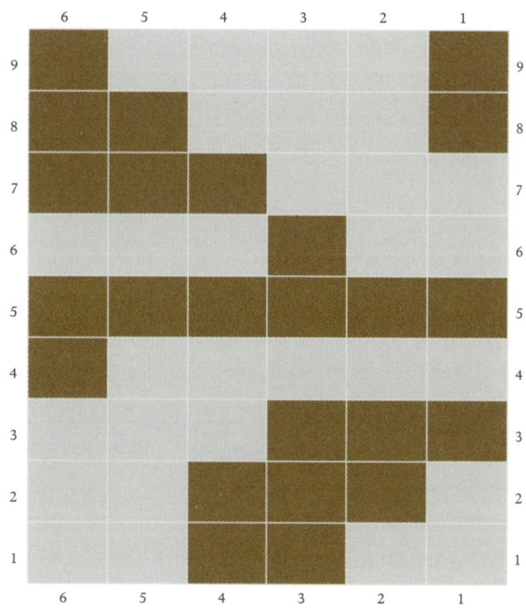


CHART A

### LEFT MITTEN

Knit as for the right mitten, but mirror the pattern by knitting all charts from left to right, instead of right to left.

Prepare for the thumb on row 16 by following chart B1: first 43 sts, then the following 11 sts with a length of yarn in a contrasting colour. Transfer these 11 sts back onto the left needle and knit them with colour 3. Then knit the last 2 stitches on the round following the chart.

**DECREASE ROW FOR TOP OF MITTEN:** SL1, k1 and pass the slipped st over the one you've just knit, and knit to last 3 sts on needle 2: K2tog, k1. Needle 3: SL1, k1 and pass the slipped st over the one you've just knit, and knit to last 3 sts on needle 4: K2tog, k1 = 4 sts decreased.

CHART B2

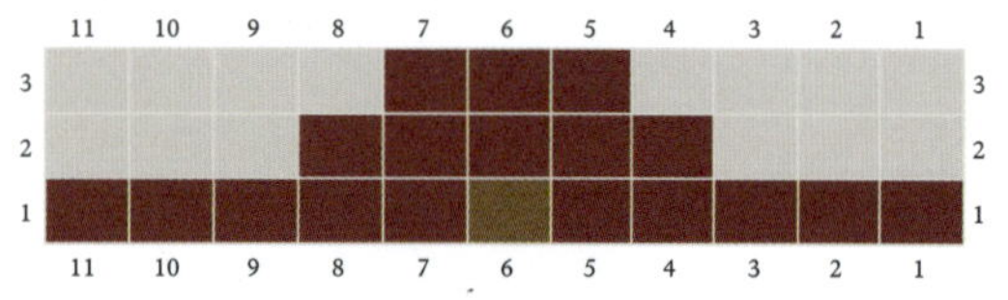

CHART B1

# Maja's mamelucker

These hotpants were born when I wanted to see if it was possible to knit old-fashioned woolly pants with a modern fit. My experiment was, to my excitement, a success and the hotpants have been knitted and appreciated by thousands of knitters. I have updated the pattern with four different sizes so that even more people can knit them!

Hotpants are perfect for wearing underneath your skirt in the winter – or why not under your ski pants when you go down the slopes? The short rows form stretchy sections at the sides, so that the woolly pants fit snugly. Keep in mind that the hotpants should have a snug fit when you first put them on, since they will stretch out a bit with use.

YARN: Järbo 2 tr ull 100% wool, 100g (3.5oz) = 300m (328yd)

TENSION: 28 sts × 40 rows in stocking stitch using 2.5mm needles = 10 × 10cm (4 × 4in)

SIZES: XS/S (M/L) XL/2XL (3XL/4XL)

FITS WAIST MEASUREMENT: 60–68 (72–84) 88–106 (112–130)cm / 23 ½–26 ¾ (28 ¼–33) 34 ¾–41 ¾ (44–51 ¼)in.

FITS HIP MEASUREMENT: 90–96 (104–110) 122–130 (142–148)cm / 35 ½–37 ¾ (41–43 ¼) 48–51 ¼ (56–58 ¼)in

AMOUNTS: 200 (200) 300 (300)g / 7.1 (7.1) 10.6 (10.6)oz Urban Blue (no. 74134)

CIRCULAR NEEDLES: 2.5mm, 40 and 60cm (16 and 24in) long

DOUBLE-POINTED NEEDLES: 2.5mm

NOTIONS: Stitch markers, 2 spare needles

DIFFICULTY LEVEL: 3 of 3

CONSTRUCTION: The hotpants are knit in the round top down in one piece – starting with a wide rib waistband, then increases and rib sections on the sides that are shaped as you go.

TECHNIQUES: PM = place marker, see Knitting School, p158.
M1B = increase 1 st in the stitch below, see Knitting School, p159.
Short rows and wrap and turn, see Knitting School, p158.

### RIB WAISTBAND

With 2.5mm circular needle, cast on 136 (160) 192 (240) sts. Work in the round in k2, p2 rib stitch until the work measures 20cm (7 ¾in).

INITIAL ROUND, SIZE XS/S ONLY: *Work in k2, p2 rib for 34 sts, k17, M1B (see Abbreviations), k17*, repeat from *–* once more = 138 sts.

### MIDDLE SECTION

ROUND 1: *Work in k2, p2 rib for 34 (38) 42 (46) st, k35 (42) 54 (74)*, repeat from *–* once more.

INCREASE ROUND A: **Place marker, *k2, p2*, repeat from *–* 7 (8) 9 (10) times, k2. PM, M1B (see Techniques) in the following 35 (42) 54 (74) sts**, repeat from **–** once more = 208 (244) 300 (388) sts.

ROUND 3: *Work in k2, p2 rib for 34 (38) 42 (46) sts, k70 (84) 108 (148)*, repeat from *–* once more.

INCREASE ROUND B: *Work in k2, p2 rib for 34 (38) 42 (46) sts, M1, k70 (84) 108 (148), M1*, repeat *–* once more (= 4 sts increased). Repeat increase round B every 5th round 6 times. NB: the new stitches are worked in stocking stitch.

REMAINING ROUNDS: Continue in established pattern with stocking stitch at front and back and rib sections on the sides.

Now a total of 7 increase round B have been made and the stitch count has increased to 236 (272) 328 (416) sts.

XS/S (34 sts in rib, 84 sts in ss) 2 times = 236 sts.

M/L (38 sts in rib, 98 sts in ss) 2 times = 272 sts.

XL/2XL (42 sts in rib, 122 sts in ss) 2 times = 328 sts.

3XL/4XL (46 sts in rib, 162 sts in ss) 2 times = 416 sts. Continue in established pattern until the work measures 11 (13) 15 (17)cm / 4 ¼ (5) 6 (6 ¾)in.

Shape the back of the hotpants using short rows (read about short rows and wrap and turn on p158 in the Knitting School). NB: remember to pick up and knit the wrapped stitches when passing them.

SHORT ROW 1 (RS): Work in k2, p2 rib for 34 (38) 42 (46) sts, k86 (100) 124 (164), p2, k1, wrap and turn.

SHORT ROW 2 (WS): P1, k2, p88 (102) 126 (166), k2, p1, wrap and turn.

SHORT ROW 3: K1, p2, k88 (102) 126 (166), p2, k2, p2, k1, wrap and turn.

SHORT ROW 4: P1, k2, p2, k2, p88 (102) 126 (166), k2, p2, k2, p1, wrap and turn.

SHORT ROW 5: K1, p2, k2, p2, k88 (102) 126 (166), (p2, k2) 2 times, p2, k1, wrap and turn.

SHORT ROW 6: P1, (k2, p2) 2 times, k2, p88 (102) 126 (166), (k2, p2) 2 times, k2, p1, wrap and turn.

SHORT ROW 7: K1, (p2, k2) 2 times, p2, k88 (102) 126 (166), (p2, k2) 3 times, p2, k1, wrap and turn.

SHORT ROW 8: P1, (k2, p2) 3 times, k2, p88 (102) 126 (166), (k2, p2) 3 times, k2, p1, wrap and turn.

SHORT ROW 9: P1, (p2, k2) 3 times, p2, k88 (102) 126 (166), (p2, k2) 4 times, p2, k1, wrap and turn.

XS/S, SHORT ROWS 10–14: Continue working in the same way and lengthen the rows by working an additional 4 sts at the end of each row.

M/L, SHORT ROWS 10–16: Continue working in the same way and lengthen the rows by working an additional 4 sts at the end of each row.

XL/2XL, SHORT ROWS 10–18: Continue working in the same way and lengthen the rows by working an additional 4 sts at the end of each row.

3XL/4XL, SHORT ROWS 10–20: Continue working in the same way and lengthen the rows by working an additional 4 sts at the end of each row.

Work one row in the round in established pattern and at the same time pick up and knit the wrapped stitches. Cut the yarn.

Leave all stitches apart from the 16 (18) 20 (22) sts in the middle of the front on the circular needle. Transfer the 16 (18) 20 (22) sts in the middle (you will then have 34 (40) 51 (70) knit stitches on each side of the rib gussets at the side) to a dpn.

### GUSSET

Work in stocking stitch back and forth until the gusset measures 9 (11) 12 (14)cm / 3 ½ (4 ¼) 4 ¾ (5 ½)in. After that you increase 1 st at each side on every other row, 6 times in total. NB: the increases should be made from the right side. Finish with a wrong side row. Now you should have 28 (30) 32 (34) sts on the dpn.

Cut the yarn but leave a length for sewing.

Transfer the other stitches to two spare needles so that you can reach the 28 (30) 32 (34) middle stitches on the back section. Transfer these stitches to a dpn.

Sew the gusset to the middle of the back section using kitchener stitch (see Knitting School, p160), which will create an invisible seam. The gusset should be attached to the back's 28 (30) 32 (34) middle stitches (there should be 28 (34) 45 (64) knit stitches on each side of the rib gussets at the sides).

## RIB EDGES

Place half of the remaining stitches on a circular needle = 96 (112) 138 (180) sts.

*Right leg*

With right side facing you, start at the centre of the gusset and pick up 12 (14) 15 (18) sts, then knit 28 (34) 45 (64) sts, 34 (38) 42 (46) in rib, knit 34 (40) 51 (70) sts and finish by picking up 12 (14) 15 (18) sts along the gusset = 120 (140) 168 (216) sts.

Knit in the round in k2, p2 rib for 12 rounds in total, or preferred length.

Cast off in rib. Cut the yarn.

*Left leg*

With right side facing you, start at the middle of the gusset and pick up 12 (14) 15 (18) sts, then knit 34 (40) 51 (70) sts, 34 (38) 42 (46) sts in rib, knit 28 (34) 45 (64) st. Finish by picking up 12 (14) 15 (18) sts along the gusset = 120 (140) 168 (216) sts.

Knit in the round in k2, p2 rib for 12 rounds in total, or matches right leg.

Cast off in rib. Cut the yarn and weave in loose ends.

# Bore

King Bore is a fairy tale figure who personifies the winter and the northern wind. As soon as the first snow falls you can see him coming on skis to spread winter and coldness around him. Sometimes he lingers far into spring, so that the humans have to light May bonfires to scare him off. Because King Bore doesn't like fire and warmth, and will then return to the north.

The Bore jumper is a classic half turtleneck jumper with a colourwork section of snowflakes on the yoke. If you are curious about colourwork knitting using two strands, this jumper is a good project to start with since the pattern has such dense colour changes that you don't have to trap the floats on the wrong side.

YARN: Léttlopi from Ístex, 100% Icelandic wool, 50g (1.8oz) = 100m (109yd)

TENSION: 18 sts × 24 rows in stocking stitch with 5mm needles = 10 × 10cm (4 × 4in)

SIZES: XS (S) M (L) XL (2XL) 3XL

JUMPER CHEST WIDTH: 86 (93) 100 (106) 113 (120) 126cm / 33 ⅓ (36 ½) 39 ½ (41 ¾) 44 ½ (47 ½) 49 ½in

JUMPER LENGTH FROM ARMHOLE: 36 (37) 38 (39) 40 (41) 42cm / 14 ¼ (14 ½) 15 (15 ¼) 15 ¾ (16 ¼) 16 ½in

SLEEVE LENGTH FROM ARMHOLE: 43 (44) 45 (46) 47 (48) 49cm / 17 (17 ¼) 17 ¾ (18) 18 ½ (19) 19 ¼in

AMOUNTS: Colour 1 = 400 (450) 450 (500) 500 (550) 550g / 14.1 (15.9) 15.9 (17.6) 17.6 (19.4) 19.4oz Air Blue (no. 1700), colour 2 = 50 (50) 50 (50) 50 (50) 50g (1.8oz) Rust Heather (no. 9427)

CIRCULAR NEEDLES: 4.5mm and 5mm, 80cm (32in) long

DOUBLE-POINTED NEEDLES: 4.5mm and 5mm

DIFFICULTY LEVEL: 2 of 3

CONSTRUCTION: The jumper's body and sleeves are knit in the round from the bottom and up. Then the sections are knit together for the yoke that is shaped with decreases.

TECHNIQUES: M1L = increase 1 st slanting left, see Knitting School, p159.
M1R = increase 1 st slanting right, see Knitting School, p159.

## BODY

With 4.5mm circular needle and colour 1, cast on 156 (168) 180 (192) 204 (216) 228 sts.

Work in the round in k1, p1 rib stitch for 5cm.

Change to 5mm circular needle and work in stocking stitch (= knit every row when knitting in the round) until the work measures 36 (37) 38 (39) 40 (41) 42cm.

FINISHING ROUND: Knit to last 5 (6) 6 (7) 7 (8) 8 sts on the round. Don't work these stitches, instead set the work aside.

## SLEEVES

With 4.5mm dpns and colour 1, cast on 38 (40) 42 (44) 46 (48) 48 sts.

Work in the round in k1, p1 rib stitch for 5cm.

Change to 5mm dpns and knit 2 rounds. NB: on the first round, increase 4 (2) 6 (4) 6 (4) 4 sts = 42 (42) 48 (48) 52 (52) 52 sts.

Work in stocking stitch in pattern following chart B, rounds 1–5 (repeat stitches 1-6 to end of round).

With colour 1, knit 2 rounds. On next round, start the sleeve increases.

INCREASE ROUND: K1, M1L (see Techniques), knit to last st on the round, M1R (see Techniques), k1.

Increase the same way every 7th (7th) 8th (7th) 7th (7th) 6th rounds, a total of 9 (11) 9 (11) 10 (12) 13 times = 60 (64) 66 (70) 72 (76) 78 sts. NB: now the increases for sizes S, L and 2XL are complete.

XS: Knit another 6 rounds and increase 1 st at the beginning of the 7th round = 61 sts.

M: Knit another 7 rounds and increase 1 st at the beginning of the 8th round = 67 sts.

XL: Knit another 6 rounds and increase 1 st at the beginning of the 7th round = 73 sts.

3XL: Knit another 5 rounds and increase 1 st at the beginning of the 6th round = 79 sts.

Knit until the sleeve measures 43 (44) 45 (46) 47 (48) 49cm / 17 (17 ¼) 17 ¾ (18) 18 ½ (19) 19 ¼in

Transfer 10 (11) 12 (13) 14 (15) 16 sts to a stitch holder. Set the work aside and knit another sleeve the same way, but mirror the chart for the second sleeve.

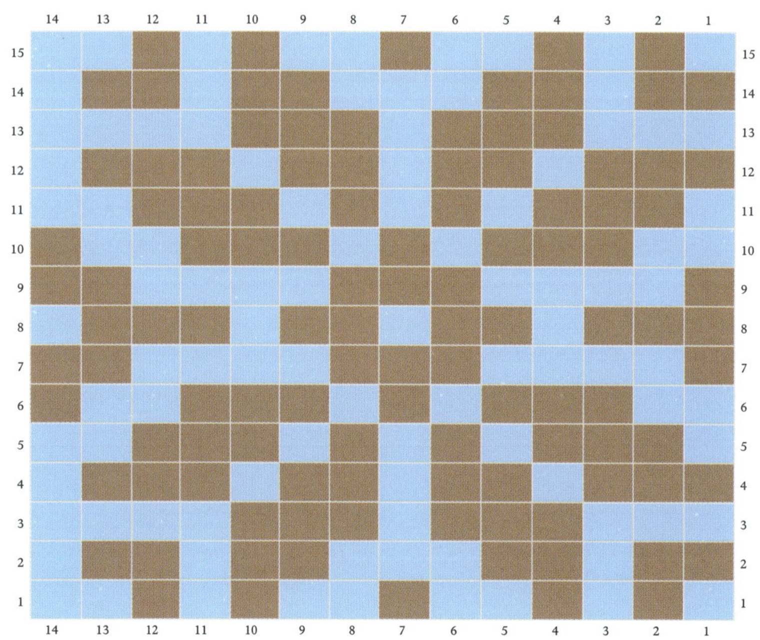

CHART A

### YOKE

Now the sections are joined for the yoke.

With 5mm circular needle and colour 1, transfer the last 5 (6) 6 (7) 7 (8) 8, as well as the first 5 (5) 6 (6) 7 (7) 8 stitches from the body to a stitch holder (= the stitches under one armhole). Knit 51 (53) 55 (57) 59 (61) 63 sleeve stitches and then 68 (73) 78 (83) 88 (93) 98 sts from the body (front). Transfer the following 10 (11) 12 (13) 14 (15) 16 sts from the body to a stitch holder (= the stitches under the other armhole). Knit the other sleeve's 51 (53) 55 (57) 59 (61) 63 sts and then 68 (73) 78 (83) 88 (93) 98 sts from the body (back). Now you will have 238 (252) 266 (280) 294 (308) 322 sts on the needle.

Knit 1 (1) 2 (2) 2 (2) 3 rounds followed by colourwork pattern following chart A, rounds 1–15 with the following placement:

XS: Knit stitch 14, repeat stitches 1–14 to last 13 sts, finish with stitches 1–13.

S: Knit stitches 3–14, repeat stitches 1–14 to last 2 sts, finish with stitches 1–2.

M: Knit stitches 12–14, repeat stitches 1–14 to last 11 sts, finish with stitches 1–11.

L: Knit stitches 8–14, repeat stitches 1–14 to last 7 sts, finish with stitches 1–7.

XL: Knit stitches 10–14, repeat stitches 1–14 to last 9 sts, finish with stitches 1–9.

2XL: Knit stitches 7–14, repeat stitches 1–14 to last 6 sts, finish with stitches 1–6.

3XL: Knit stitches 8–14, repeat stitches 1–14 to last 7 sts, finish with stitches 1–7.

With colour 1, knit 2 rounds.

*Decrease round 1*

XS AND L: K4, SL1, k1 and pass the slipped st over the one you've just knitted, k2, *k3, k2tog, k5, SL1, k1 and pass the slipped st over the one you've just knitted, k2*, repeat from *–* to last 6 sts on the round, k3, k2tog, k1.

S AND XL: K1, k2tog, k5, SL1, k1 and pass the slipped st over the one you've just knitted, k2, *k3, k2tog, k5, SL1, k1 and pass the slipped st over the one you've just knitted, k2*, repeat from *–* to last 2 sts on the round, k2.

M AND 2XL: K2, *k3, k2tog, k5, SL1, k1 and pass the slipped st over the one you've just knitted, k2*, repeat from *–* to last 12 sts on the round, k3, k2tog, k5, SL1, k1 and pass the slipped st over the one you've just knitted.

3XL: K3, SL1, k1 and pass the slipped st over the one you've just knitted. K2, *k3, k2tog, k5, SL1, k1 and pass the slipped st over the one you've just knitted, k2*, repeat from *–* to last 7 sts on the round, k3, k2tog, k2.

After decrease round 1, you will have 204 (216) 228 (240) 252 (264) 276 sts on the needle.

Knit 7 (8) 8 (9) 10 (10) 10 rounds.

*Decrease round 2*

XS AND L: K1, k2tog, k4, *k2tog, k4, k2tog, k4*, repeat from *–* to last 5 sts on the round, k2tog, k3.

S AND XL: K4, k2tog, k4, *k2tog, k4, k2tog, k4*. Repeat from *–* to last 2 sts on the round, k2tog.

M AND 2XL: K2, *k2tog, k4, k2tog, k4*, repeat from *–* to last 10 sts on the round, k2tog, k4, k2tog, k2.

3XL: K2tog, k4, *k2tog, k4, k2tog, k4*, repeat from *–* to last 6 sts on the round, k2tog, k4.

After decrease round 2 you will have 170 (180) 190 (200) 210 (220) 230 sts on the needle.

Knit 9 (9) 9 (10) 10 (10) 10 rounds.

*Decrease round 3*

XS AND L: K2tog, k3, *k2tog, k3, k2tog, k3*, repeat from *–* to last 5 sts in the round, k2tog, k3.

S AND XL: K3, k2tog, k3, *k2tog, k3, k2tog, k3*, repeat from *–* to last 2 sts on the round, k2tog.

M AND 2XL: K1, *k2tog, k3, k2tog, k3*, repeat from *–* to last 9 sts on the round, k2tog, k3, k2tog, k2.

3XL: K2tog, k3, *k2tog, k3, k2tog, k3*, repeat from *–* to last 5 sts on the round, k2tog, k3.

After decrease round 3 you will have 136 (144) 152 (160) 168 (176) 184 sts on the needle.

Knit 4 (4) 5 (5) 5 (5) 6 rounds.

*Decrease round 4*

XS AND L: K2, k2tog, *k2tog, k2, k2tog, k2*, repeat from *–* to last 4 sts on the round, k2, k2tog.

S AND XL: K1, k2tog, k2, k2tog, *k2tog, k2, k2tog, k2*, repeat from *–* to last st on the round, k1.

M AND 2XL: K2tog, *k2tog, k2, k2tog, k2*, repeat from *–* to last 6 sts on the round, k2, k2tog, k2.

3XL: K2, k2tog, *k2tog, k2, k2tog, k2*, repeat from *–* to last 4 sts on the round, k2, k2tog.

After decrease round 4 you will have 102 (108) 114 (120) 126 (132) 138 sts on the needle.

Knit 2 rounds.

*Decrease round 5*

XS AND L: K1, k2tog, *k1, k2tog, k1, k2tog*, repeat from *–* to last 3 sts on the round, k1, k2tog.

S AND XL: K2tog, k1, k2tog, *k1, k2tog, k1, k2tog*, repeat from *–* to last st on the round, k1.

M AND 2XL: K2tog, *k1, k2tog, k1, k2tog*, repeat from *–* to last 4 sts on the round, k1, k2tog, k1.

3XL: k1, k2tog, *k1, k2tog, k1, k2tog*, repeat from *–* to last 3 sts on the round, k1, k2tog.

After decrease round 5 you will have 68 (72) 76 (80) 84 (88) 92 sts on the needle.

SIZES XL, 2XL AND 3XL: Knit 1 round.

## TURTLENECK

Change to 4.5mm circular needle and knit 1 round and at the same time decrease 0 (0) 2 (6) 8 (10) 12 sts evenly spaced over the round = 68 (72) 74 (74) 76 (78) 80 sts.

Work in k1, p1 rib for 8cm (3 1/4in)

Cast off loosely.

## FINISHING

Join the stitches under the armholes using the 3-needle cast off technique, see Knitting School, p160.

Weave in loose ends. Block the jumper carefully following the measurements specified and instructions in the Knitting School, p156.

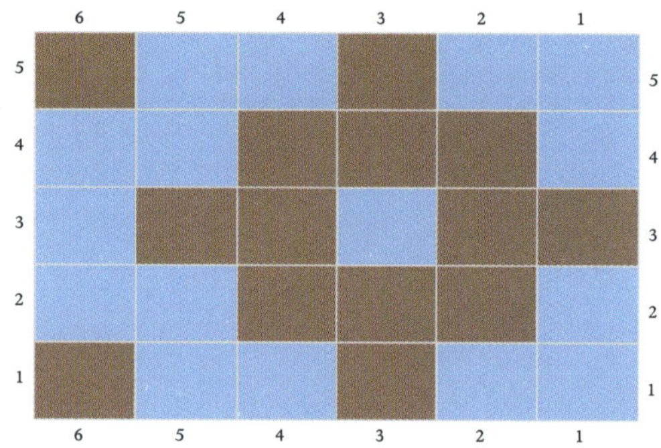


CHART B

# Sheaf

Christmas sheafs have been put up in the Nordic countries since the 18th century, but the tradition probably goes back further than that. But putting them up, people hoped that the garden birds would fill up and stay away from the fields over the coming year.

In the west of Sweden, they held the belief that the sheaf was for the Norse god Thor's goats. It should therefore be put up on a tall rod to protect against lightning strikes. The Sheaf socks are knitted in classic sock yarn with a grain-like pattern on the garter-stitched legs.

YARN: Raggi, 70% superwash wool, 30% polyamide, 100g (3.5oz) = 150m (164yd)

TENSION: 18 sts × 23 rows in stocking stitch using 4mm needles = 10 × 10cm (4 × 4in)

SIZES: UK 1/2 (3/4) 5/6 (7/8) 9/10 (11/12) / EU 34/35 (36/37) 38/39 (40/41) 42/43 (44/45)

SOCK CIRCUMFERENCE: 19 (19) 21 (21) 23 (23)cm / 7 ½ (7 ½) 8 ¼ (8 ¼) 9 (9)in

SOCK LENGTH: 21.5 (23) 24.5 (25.5) 27 (28)cm / 8 ½ (9) 9 ½ (10) 10 ½ (11)in

AMOUNTS: Colour 1 = 100 (100) 100 (150) 150 (150)g / 3.5 (3.5) 3.5 (5.3) 5.3 (5.3)oz Morel Brown (no. 15117)

DOUBLE-POINTED NEEDLES: 4mm and 4.5mm

NOTIONS: 4 stitch markers

DIFFICULTY LEVEL: 2 of 3

CONSTRUCTION: The socks are knit from the toe up with a classic heel for toe-up socks.

TECHNIQUES: Judy's magic cast on, see video links in the Knitting School on p160.

M1L = increase 1 st slanting left, see Knitting School, p159.

M1R = increase 1 st slanting right, see Knitting School, p159.

Cable k3tog right = Place 2 sts on a cable needle at the back of the work. Knit together the following 3 sts, knit the 2 sts on the cable needle.

Cable k3tog left = Place 3 sts on a cable needle at the front of the work. Knit the following 2 sts, knit together the 3 sts on the cable needle through the back loop.

Short rows and wrap and turn: see Knitting School, p158.

### TOE

With 4mm dpns and colour 1, cast on 14 (14) 18 (18) 22 (22) sts evenly spaced over two needles using the Judy's magic cast on technique (see Techniques).

ROUND 1: Knit and at the same time divide the stitches evenly over four needles.

ROUND 2: K1, M1L (see Techniques), knit to last st on needle 2, M1R (see Techniques), k1. Needle 3: K1, M1L, knit to last st on needle 4, M1R, k1.

Repeat rounds 1 and 2 until you have a total of 38 (38) 42 (42) 46 (46) sts.

Stitches 1–19 (1–19) 1–21 (1–21) 1–23 (1–23) = top. Stitches 20–38 (20–38) 22–42 (22–42) 24–46 (24–46) = bottom.

### FOOT

Knit 2 rounds.

Work in stocking stitch until the foot measures 12 (13.5) 14.5 (15.5) 17 (18)cm / 4 ¾ (5 ¼) 5 ¾ (6) 6 ¾ (7)in

### GUSSET

ROUND 1: Top: Knit. Bottom: K1, M1L, knit to last st, M1R, k1.

ROUND 2: Knit.

Repeat rounds 1–2 until you have 31 (31) 33 (33) 35 (35) sts at the bottom.

Knit another round and then knit across the stitches at the top. Now it's time to knit the heel.

### HEEL

The heel is knitted back and forth using short rows and wrapped stitches (read about short rows and wrap and turn on p158 in the Knitting School). Now we only work with the stitches at the bottom/back. Place 4 markers as follows:

M1 after the 6th (6 th) 6 th (6 th) 6 th (6 th) st.

M2 after the 11 th (11 th) 11 th (11 th) 12 th (12 th) st.

M3 after the 20 th (20th) 22nd (22nd) 23rd (23rd) st.

M4 after the 25 th (25th) 27 th (27 th) 29 th (29 th) st.

Between M1 and M4 you have the middle 19 (19) 21 (21) 23 (23) sts which will become the heel flap.

Between M2 and M3 you have the middle 9 (9) 11 (11) 11 (11) sts which will become centre back at the heel tip.

ROW 1 (RS): Knit to last st before M4, wrap and turn.

ROW 2 (WS): Purl to last st before M1, wrap and turn.

ROW 3 (RS): Knit to last st before the turning stitch from the previous row, wrap and turn.

ROW 4 (WS): Purl to last st before the turning stitch from the previous row, wrap and turn.

Repeat rows 3 and 4 until all stitches outside M2 and M3 have been wrapped. The middle 9 (9) 11 (11) 11 (11) sts, between M2 and M3, shall not be wrapped.

FOLLOWING ROW (RS): K9 (9) 11 (11) 11 (11). Knit all wrapped stitches until M4. Turn.

NEXT ROW (WS): SL1 purlwise, purl until you reach the wrapped stitches (after M2). Purl all wrapped stitches until M1.

### HEEL FLAP

At the same time as the straight heel flap is worked you knit the gusset's stiches together with the sides of the heel flap.

ROW 1 (RS): Turn and SL1 knitwise at the same time as you hold the yarn taut, knit to last st before M4, k2tog tbl.

ROW 2 (WS): Turn and SL1 purlwise at the same time as you hold the yarn taut, purl to last st before M1, remove the stitch marker, p2tog. Remove remaining stitch markers.

ROW 3 (RS): Turn and SL1 knitwise (hold the yarn taut), knit until you reach the slipped stitch.

Knit the slipped stitch together with the next stitch from the gusset: k2tog tbl (= 1 st before + 1 st after the small gap that has formed at the turning).

ROW 4 (WS): Turn and SL1 purlwise (hold the yarn taut), purl until you reach the slipped stitch. Purl the slipped stitch together with the next stitch from the gusset: p2tog (= 1 st before + 1 st after the gap).

Repeat rows 3–4 until your run out of gusset stitches (after knitting together on a RS row). Work to end of row.

NEXT ROW: Top: Knit. Bottom/back: k2tog, k18 (18) 20 (20) 22 (22).

Now the heel is finished and you will have the same number of stitches as you did before working the heel.

## LEG

Change to 4.5mm dpns. Knit 1 round and at the same time increase (1) (0) 0 (2) 2 sts evenly spaced over the round = 39 (39) 42 (42) 48 (48) sts.

Thereafter the leg is worked in garter stitch with a grain motif, as follows:

ROUND 1: *K2, [k1, yo, k1] in the same stitch, k1, [k1, yo, k1] in the same stitch, k2, p6 (6) 7 (7) 9 (9)*, repeat from *–* 2 times.

ROUND 2: *K2, [Sl3 knitwise from left to right needle, k1, sl3 sts from left to right needle], k2, 6 (6) 7 (7) 9 (9)*, repeat from *–* 2 times.

ROUND 3: (Cables, see Techniques) *[Cable k3tog right, k1, cable k3tog left], k1, [cable k3tog right, k1, cable k3tog left], p6 (6) 7 (7) 9 (9)*. Repeat from *–* 2 times.

ROUND 4: *k3, SL1 from left to right needle, k3, 6 (6) 7 (7) 9 (9)*, repeat from *–* 2 times.

Repeat rounds 1–4 a total of 10 times. The leg will then measure approximately 10cm (4in).

Cast off med liksidig avmaskning (see video links in the Knitting School p160) and cut the yarn. Weave in loose ends. Knit one more sock the same way.

# Juniper

Juniper is a plant with many uses that grows all over the country, and the spiky needles were said to protect against danger and evil. They are positioned three and three, like the holy trinity – which was thought to have given the juniper tree its magical powers.

Another explanation could be that the cross-like pattern that can be found underneath each berry is said to depict Thor's hammer or the cross of Christ.

In the past, juniper berry drink was served at winter festivities. This tradition is still alive in Värmland, where I live. The juniper berry drink is made from dried juniper berries that are picked in the autumn, among other things.

The Juniper cardigan is a warm and rustic cardigan that is embellished with a juniper pattern both at the top on the yoke and the bottom on the cuffs.

YARN: Álafosslopi from Ístex, 100% Icelandic wool, 100g (3.5oz) = 100m (109yd)

TENSION: 13 sts × 18 rows in stocking stitch in pattern with 6mm needles = 10 × 10cm (4 ×4in)

SIZES: XS (S) M (L) XL (2XL) 3XL

CARDIGAN CHEST WIDTH: 84 (90) 99 (104) 112 (118) 124cm / 33 (35 ½) 40 (41) 44 (45 ½) 48 ½in

CARDIGAN LENGTH FROM ARMHOLE: 25 (26) 27 (28) 29 (30) 31cm / 9 ¾ (10 ¼) 10 ½ (11) 11½ (11 ¾) 12 ¼in

SLEEVE LENGTH FROM ARMHOLE: 44 (45) 46 (47) 48 (49) 50cm / 17 ¼ (17 ¾) 18 (18 ½) 19 (19 ½) 19 ¾in

AMOUNTS: Colour 1 = 500 (500) 500 (500) 600 (600) 700g / 17.6 (17.6) 17.6 (17.6) 21.2 (21.2) 24.7oz Oxblood Red (no. 1242), colour 2 = 200 (200) 200 (200) 200 (200) 200g / 7.1oz Chartreuse Green Heather (no. 9965), colour 3 = 200 (200) 200 (200) 200 (200) 200g / 7.1oz Ecru Heather (no. 9972), colour 4 = 100 (100) 100 (100) 100 (100) 100g / 3.5oz Indigo (no. 9959)

CIRCULAR NEEDLES: 4.5mm and 6mm, 80cm (32in) long

DOUBLE-POINTED NEEDLES: 4.5mm and 6mm

NOTIONS: 5 buttons, 20mm (0.8in) in diameter

DIFFICULTY LEVEL: 3 of 3

CONSTRUCTION: Body and sleeves are knit in the round separately from the bottom up and are then placed on the same circular needle. Then the yoke is knit with decreases, short rows at the back and a neckband. To finish, button bands are knit on and the cardigan is cut open (see Knitting School, p154).

## BODY

With 4.5mm circular needle and colour 1, cast on 97 (105) 115 (121) 131 (135) 139 sts. Now the rib is worked back and forth.

ROW 1 (WS): *P1, k1*, repeat from *–* to last st, p1.

ROW 2 (RS): *K1, p1*, repeat from *–* to last st, k1.

Repeat rows 1 and 2 until the rib measures 7cm (2 ¾in). Ending with a WS row.

Change to 6mm circular needle.

Knit one row and at the same time increase 8 (9) 10 (11) 12 (15) 18 sts evenly spaced over the row = 105 (114) 125 (132) 143 (150) 157 sts.

NB: at the end of the row cast on 3 new steek stitches using the double twisted loop technique (see video links in the Knitting School on p160). These stitches are not included in the total stitch count and no decreases or increases should be made in these stitches.

Continue working in the round in stocking stitch (= knit all stitches when working in the round).

Knit until the work measures 25 (26) 27 (28) 29 (30) 31cm / 9 ¾ (10 ¼) 10 ½ (11) 11 ½ (11 ¾) 12 ¼in

Set the work aside.

## SLEEVES

With 4.5mm dpns and colour 2, cast on 30 (30) 30 (32) 32 (34) 36 sts.

Work in the round in k1, p1 rib stitch for 7cm (2 ¾in).

Change to 6mm dpns.

Knit 1 round. NB: at the same time increase 18 (18) 18 (16) 16 (14) 12 sts = 48 (48) 48 (48) 48 (48) 48 sts.

Knit the colourwork pattern in stocking stitch following chart B, rounds 1–16 (repeat stitches 1–12 to end of round).

With colour 1, knit 2 rounds.

On the following round, decrease/increase as follows.

XS, S, M: Decrease 5 (3) 1 (0) 0 (0) 0 sts evenly spaced over the round.

L, XL, 2XL AND 3XL: Increase 0 (0) 0 (3) 5 (9) 13 sts evenly spaced over the round.

Now you will have 43 (45) 47 (51) 53 (57) 61 sts on the needle.

Knit until the sleeve measures 44 (45) 46 (47) 48 (49) 50cm / 17 ¼ (17 ¾) 18 (18 ½) 19 (19 ½) 19 ¾in.

Transfer 6 (7) 8 (9) 10 (11) 12 sts to a stitch holder. Set the work aside and knit one more sleeve the same way.

## YOKE

Now body and sleeves are joined together to form the yoke.

With 6mm circular needle and colour 1: knit right front's 23 (25) 27 (28) 31 (32) 33 sts, transfer the following 7 (7) 8) (9) 10 (11) 12 sts to a stitch holder or length of scrap yarn. Knit the first sleeve's 37 (38) 39 (42) 43 (46) 49 sts, the back's 45 (50) 55 (58) 61 (64) 67 sts and then transfer the following 7 (7) 8 (9) 10 (11) 12 sts to a stitch holder or length of scrap yarn.

Knit the other sleeve's 37 (38) 39 (42) 43 (46) 49 sts followed by the left front's 23 (25) 27 (28) 31 (32) 33 sts = 165 (176) 187 (198) 209 (220) 231 sts.

Knit colourwork pattern in stocking stitch and decrease following chart A with placement as described below.

XS, S, M: Work rounds 1–6 as follows, *stitches 1–17, then repeat stitches 7–17 a total of 13 (14) 15 (0) 0 (0) 0 times, then finish the round with stitches 18–22*. (Skip rounds 7–11). Work rounds 12–43, repeat from *–*.

L, XL, 2XL AND 3XL: Work rounds 1–43 as follows, stitches 1–17, then repeat stitches 7–17 a total of 0 (0) 0 (16) 17 (18) 19 times, then finish the round with stitches 18–22.

When the chart is finished you will have 61 (65) 69 (73) 77 (81) 85 sts on the needle.

## NECKBAND

Change to 4.5mm circular needle.

INITIAL ROUND: With colour 1, decrease 10 (12) 16 (18) 20 (24) 28 sts evenly spaced over the round. NB: at the end of the round the 3 steek stitches are cast off.

Work back and forth in k1, p1 rib for 8cm (3 ¼in), ending with a WS round.

Cast off loosely in rib.

CHART A

No stitch ⁄ Decrease 1 st slanting right ⟍ Decrease 1 st slanting left

## BUTTON BANDS

*Left button band*

With 4.5mm circular needle and colour 1 (RS), pick up stitches along the left front edge starting at the top. To ensure the edge has the right amount of stretch you pick up 3 of 4 sts (= *pick up 3 sts, skip the 4th st*, repeat from *–*). Make sure that the stitch count is odd.

Now work in rib.

ROW 1 (WS): *P1, k1*, repeat from *–* to last st, p1.

ROW 2 (RS): *K1, p1*, repeat from *–* to last st, k1.

ROW 3 (WS): *P1, k1*, repeat from *–* to last st, p1.

Repeat rows 2 and 3 a total of 3 times (= 7 rows in total). Cast off in rib.

*Right button band*

With 4.5mm circular needle and colour 1 (RS): Pick up stitches along the right front edge starting at the bottom. Make sure to pick up the same number of stitches as for the left button band.

Divide 5 buttonholes evenly over the button band. (Each buttonhole goes over 2 sts.)

Work in rib following instructions for left button band until row 3.

ROW 4 (BUTTONHOLE ROW, RS): Work in established rib until the first buttonhole. Then work as follows: *K2tog, yo, continue in established rib until next buttonhole*, repeat from *–* until all buttonholes have been started and then work in rib to end of row.

Work 3 rows in rib and then cast off in rib.

*Cutting the steek*

See Knitting School, p154. Sew a reinforcing seam with sewing thread (by hand using backstitch) on each side of the middle steek stitch. Carefully cut the cardigan open in the middle of the middle steek stitch. (The cut edges will roll in towards the wrong side.)

## FINISHING

Fold the neckband double against the wrong side and carefully sew it in place using whip stitches. Sew together the holes under the armholes using kitchener stitch (see Knitting School, p160).

Weave in loose ends. Block the cardigan carefully, following the measurements specified and instructions in the Knitting School, p156.

Sew on buttons level with the buttonholes. Either cover the cut edges on the inside with a decorative band (see Knitting School, p155), or fold them in and sew with discreet stitches to the wrong side.

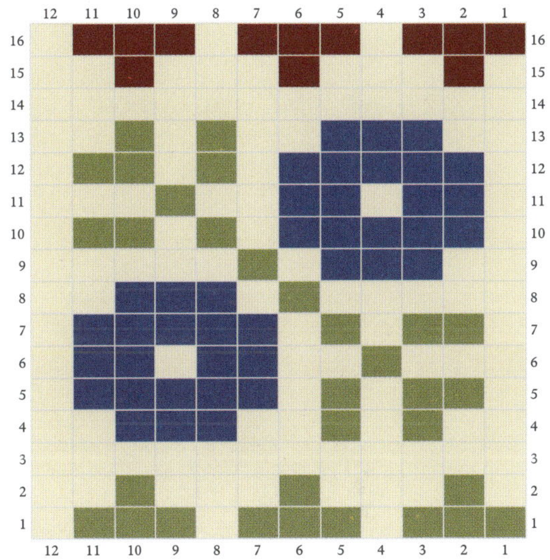


CHART B

# Forne

During winter evenings, in the light from the wood burner, I can sometimes feel the presence of years gone by. It's easy imagine how people in former times also came closer to the fire, listened to the comforting crackle, and came together both for quiet time and for conversation.

A garment knitted in colourwork has the benefit, besides being beautiful, of being warmer than a single-colour one, thanks to the double strands that run across the wrong side of the garment. For this reason, colourwork with two or three strands are common in the Nordic region.

The Forne jumper is based on a traditional, densely-knit design. You can personalise your jumper with date and initials, if you want. See the alphabet chart on p161. You'll also find a blank chart on p115 where you can draw your own initials, if you'd prefer that.

The matching hat is perfect if you want to try to knit the colourwork pattern in a smaller format. Then you can use that as your 'test swatch' to check your tension while practicing two-strand colourwork at the same time.

# Jumper

YARN: Järbo 2 trull, 100% wool, 100g (3.5oz) = 300m (328yd)

TENSION: 24 sts × 31 rows in stocking stitch in pattern with 3.5mm needles = 10 × 10cm (4 × 4in)

SIZES: XXS (XS) S (M) L (XL) 2XL (3XL) 4XL (5XL)

JUMPER CHEST WIDTH: 85 (90) 95 (105) 110 (115) 120 (125) 130 (140)cm / 33 ½ (35 ⅓) 37 ½ (41 ¼) 43 ¼ (45 ¼) 47 ¼ (49 ¼) 51 ¼ (55 ¼)in

JUMPER LENGTH: 57 (58) 61 (62) 63 (65) 66 (70) 73 (77)cm / 22 ½ (22 ¾) 24 (24 ½) 24 ¾ (25 ½) 26 (27 ½) 28 ¾ (30 ¼)in

JUMPER SLEEVE LENGTH: 47 (48) 49 (50) 51 (52) 52 (53) 53 (54)cm / 18 ½ (19) 19 ¼ (19 ¾) 20 (20 ½) 20 ½ (20 ¾) 20 ¾ (21 ¼)in

AMOUNTS: Colour 1 = 250 (250) 250 (300) 300 (350) 350 (400) 400 (450)g / 8.8 (8.8) 8.8 (10.6) 10.6 (12.3) 12.3 (14.1) 14.1 (15.9)oz, Silver Stream (no. 74104), colour 2 = 200 (250) 250 (300) 300 (350) 350 (400) 400 (450)g / 7.1 (8.8) 8.8 (10.6) 10.6 (12.3) 12.3 (14.1) 14.1 (15.9)oz, Cranberry Red (no. 74122)

CIRCULAR NEEDLES: 3mm and 3.5mm, 40cm (16in) and 80cm (32in) long

DOUBLE-POINTED NEEDLES: 3mm and 3.5mm

NOTIONS: 4 stitch markers

DIFFICULTY LEVEL: 3 of 3

CONSTRUCTION: The jumper is knit from the bottom up, then the yoke is shaped with help from raglan decreases.

TECHNIQUES: K2tog tbl = 2 twisted knit stitches together. Slip 2 stitches knitwise, transfer the stitches back onto the left needle and purl together through the back loop.

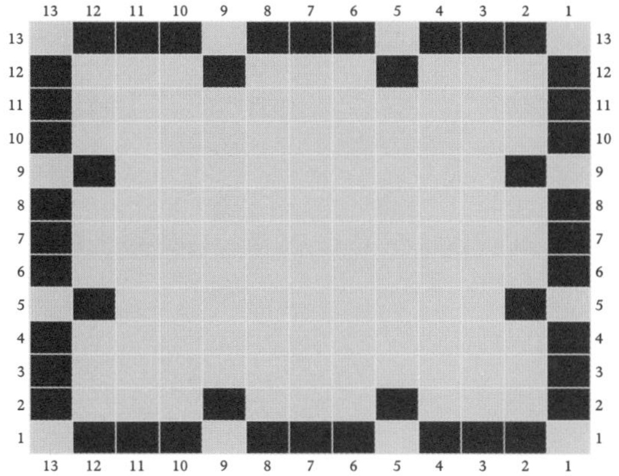


## BODY

With 3mm circular needle and colour 1, cast on 204 (216) 228 (252) 264 (276) 288 (300) 312 (336) sts.

Work in the round in k1, p1 rib stitch for 6cm (2 ½in).

Change to 3.5mm circular needle and work 2 rounds in stocking stitch (= knit every row when knitting in the round). NB: on the first round increase 4 (0) 4 (4) 0 (4) 0 (4) 0 (0) sts = 208 (216) 232 (256) 264 (280) 288 (304) 312 (336) sts.

Place a stitch marker to mark the beginning of the round and then one more after half the round to divide the stitches with 104 (108) 116 (128) 132 (140) 144 (152) 156 (168) sts for the front and back.

Knit pattern following the chart, rounds 1–8 (stitches 1–8 are repeated to end of round).

Repeat the pattern until the body measures 38 (39) 40 (40) 40 (41) 42 (42) 43 (44) cm, or preferred length.

Cast off 5 (4) 5 (5) 4 (5) 4 (5) 4 (4) sts before and after the markers at the jumper's sides. = 20 (16) 20 (20) 16 (20) 16 (20) 16 (16) sts decreased in total. Now you will have 188 (200) 212 (236) 248 (260) 272 (284) 296 (320) sts on the needle.

Set the work aside and make the sleeves.

## SLEEVES

NB: if you want to add a knitted monogram to the sleeves (see overleaf) they should be placed in the middle of the sleeve after the first 11 rows of stocking stitch.

With 3mm dpns and colour 1, cast on 48 (48) 48 (52) 52 (56) 56 (56) 60 (60) sts.

Work in the round in k1, p1 rib stitch for 6cm (2 ½in).

Change to 3.5mm dpns and knit 2 rounds in stocking stitch. NB: on the first round increase 6 (6) 6 (8) 8 (8) 10 (10) 12 (14) sts evenly spaced over the row = 54 (54) 54(60) 60 (64) 66 (66) 72 (74) sts.

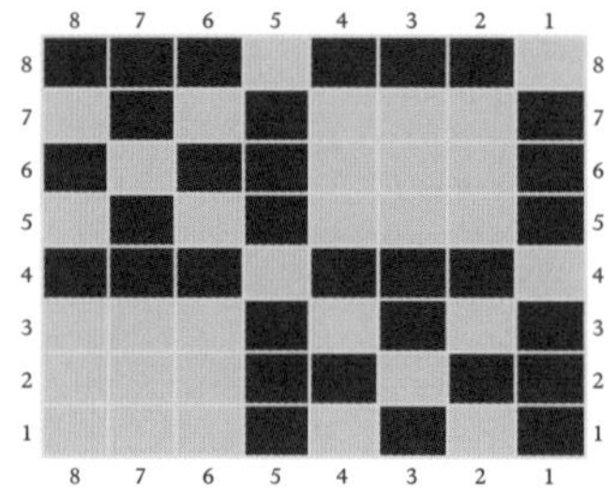

Place a stitch marker to mark the beginning of the round. The first st after the marker is the middle stitch (at the bottom of the armhole) The middle stitch as well as the stitch before and after are always worked with colour 1.

NB: these 3 stitches (the middle stitch and the 2 stitches on each side) are not included in the colourwork pattern.

Knit pattern following the chart (= start with stitch 8 (8) 8 (1) 1 (7) 6 (6) 7 (6) in the chart) and at the same time increase 1 st on each side of the middle stitch every 2 (2.5) 2 (2) 2.5 (2) 1.5 (1.5) 2 (2)cm / ¾ (1) ¾ (¾) 1 (¾) ½ (½) ¾ (¾)in gap, until you have 82 (84) 90 (92) 94 (96) 100 (108) 116 (122) sts in total on the needle.

NB: the increase should be worked with colour 1.

Then continue knit in established pattern until the sleeves measure 47 (48) 49 (50) 51 (52) 52 (53) 53 (54)cm / 18 ½ (19) 19 ¼ (19 ¾) 20 (20 ½) 20 ½ (20 ¾) 20 ¾ (21 ¼)in, or preferred length.

Cast off 5 (4) 5 (5) 4 (5) 4 (5) 4 (4) sts before and after the marker at the middle under the armhole (= 10 (8) 10 (10) 8 (10) 8 (10) 8 (8) sts decreased in total). Now you will have 72 (76) 80 (82) 86 (86) 92 (98) 108 (114) sts on the needle.

Set the work aside and knit one more sleeve the same way.

### YOKE

Add the sleeves to the same needle as the body and place four stitch markers where sleeve and body meet. You will now have 332 (352) 372 (400) 420 (432) 456 (480) 512 (548) sts on the needle.

The first and the last stitch on the sleeves are raglan stitches (= 4 raglan stitches in total). It's here

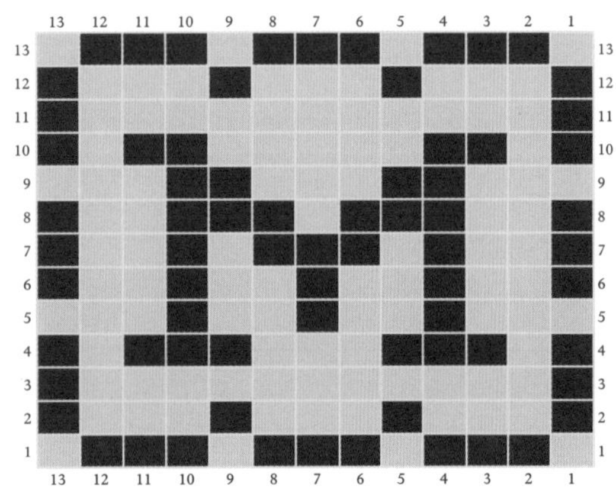

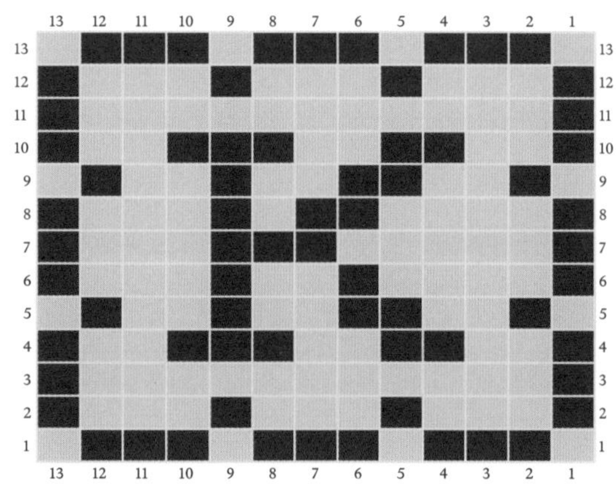

If you want to add a monogram on your jumper you can use these letter charts or draw up your own. See blank chart on previous page and letters on p161.

the raglan decreases will be made at the same time as the chart is continued. The chart is not even, instead it will be cut off at each raglan decrease. Make sure that the pattern matches up with previously knitted pattern on body and sleeves.

Knit 10 (6) 6 (4) 4 (4) 4 (2) 2 (2) rounds before you start with the raglan decreases.

Raglan decrease: (NB: 1 st before and after each raglan stitch is always worked with colour 1, the raglan stitches are also worked with colour 1.)

*Knit the raglan stitch, k2tog tbl with colour 1, knit to last 2 sts before the next raglan stitch, k2tog with colour 1, knit the raglan stitch, k2tog tbl with colour 1, continue to knit in colourwork pattern to last 2 sts before the next raglan stitch, k2tog with colour 1*. Repeat from *–* once more = 8 sts decreased.

Knit one round without decreases.

Continue making the raglan decreases every other round a total of 25 (27) 27 (26) 26 (26) 25 (23) 21 (16) times = 132 (136) 156 (192) 212 (224) 256 (296) 344 (420) sts.

Make raglan decreases on every round 0 (0) 2 (6) 8 (10) 14 (20) 24 (34) times = 132 (136) 140 (144) 148 (144) 144 (136) 152 (148) sts.

### NECKBAND

Knit one round with colour 1 and evenly decrease 28 (32) 32 (30) 30 (22) 22 (14) 30 (26) sts = 104 (104) 108 (114) 118 (122) 122 (122) 122 (122) sts.

Change to 3mm circular needle and work 4cm (1 ½in) k1, p1 rib. Purl one round = folded edge.

Work another 4cm (1 ½in) in rib.

Cast off loosely. Fold in the edge of the neckband and sew into place on the wrong side with discreet whip stitches.

### FINISHING

Weave in loose ends.

Block the cardigan carefully following the measurements specified and instructions in the Knitting School, p156.

# Hat

YARN: Fjallalopi from Ístex, 100% Icelandic wool, 50g (1.8oz) = 150m (164yd)

TENSION: 24 sts × 31 rows in stocking stitch in pattern with 4mm needles = 10 × 10 cm (4 × 4 in)

SIZES: S (M) L

HEAD CIRCUMFERENCE: 50–52 (53–55) 56–58cm / 19 ¾–20 ½ (20 ¾–21 ¾) (22–22 ¾)in

HAT CIRCUMFERENCE: 40 (43) 47cm / 15 ¾ (17) 18 ½in (unstretched)

HAT TOTAL LENGTH: 27 (28) 29cm / 10 ¾ (11) 11 ½in

HAT LENGTH: 21 (22) 23cm / 8 ¼ (8 ¾) 9in (folded)

AMOUNTS: Colour 1 = 40 (50) 60g / 1.4 (1.8) 2.1oz Light Moorit (no. 13001), colour 2 = 30 (30) 40g / 1 (1) 1.4oz Gravel Grey (no. 13058)

CIRCULAR NEEDLES: 3.5mm and 4mm, 40cm (16in) long

DOUBLE-POINTED NEEDLES: 4mm

DIFFICULTY LEVEL: 2 of 3

CONSTRUCTION: The hat is knit in the round from the bottom up, with a cuffed rib and a colourwork section that is finished with decreases.

### CUFF

With 3.5mm circular needle and colour 1, cast on 92 (100) 108 sts.

Work in the round in k1, p1 rib stitch for 12 (13) 14cm / 4 ¾ (5) 5 ½in.

### COLOURWORK SECTION

With 4mm circular needle, knit 1 round and at the same time increase 4 sts evenly spaced over the round = 96 (104) 112 sts.

Knit colourwork pattern in stocking stitch (= knit every round when knitting in the round) following the chart, rounds 1–8 (NB: rounds 1–8 are repeated to end of round). Repeat rounds 1–8 another 2 times.

With colour 1, knit until the work measures 22 (23) 24cm / 8 ¾ (9) 9 ½in.

## CROWN

Knit 2 rounds (NB: for size M, decrease 8 sts evenly spaced over the first of the 2 rounds = 96 (96) 112 sts).

DECREASE ROUND 1: *K1, SL1, k1 and pass the slipped st over the one you've just knit, k6 (6) 8, k2tog, k1*, repeat from *–* to end of round = 16 sts decreased = 80 (80) 96 sts.

Knit 1 round. (Change to 4mm dpns when the circumference of the hat requires it.)

DECREASE ROUND 2: *K1, SL1, k1 and pass the slipped st over the one you've just knitted, k4 (4) 6, k2tog, k1*, repeat from *–* to end of round = 16 sts decreased = 64 (64) 80 sts.

Knit 1 round.

DECREASE ROUND 3: *K1, SL1, k1 and pass the slipped st over the one you've just knitted. K2 (2) 4, k2tog, k1*. Repeat from *–* to end of round = 16 sts decreased = 48 (48) 64 sts.

Knit 1 round.

DECREASE ROUND 4: *K1, SL1, k1 and pass the slipped st over the one you've just knitted, k0 (0) 2, k2tog, k1*, repeat from *–* to end of round = 16 sts decreased = 32 (32) 48 sts.

Knit 1 round. NB: only work decrease round 5 for size L.

DECREASE ROUND 5: *K1, SL1, k1 and pass the slipped st over the one you've just knitted, k2tog, k1*, repeat from *–* to end of round = 16 sts decreased = - (-) 32 sts.

Knit 1 round.

*Final decrease round for all sizes*

ROUND 1: *K1, k2tog, k1*, repeat from *–* to end of round = 8 sts decreased = 24 (24) 24 sts.

Knit 1 round.

ROUND 2: *K2tog*, repeat from *–* to end of round = 12 (12) 12 sts.

Cut the yarn, pass through the end of the yarn and secure in place.

## FINISHING

Weave in loose ends. Block the hat carefully following the measurements specified and instructions in the Knitting School, p156.

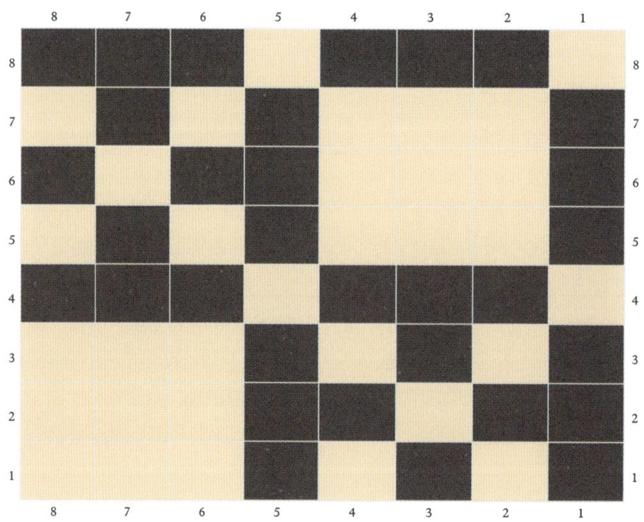

# Black Magic

Books on black magic can be found in the collection of Nordiska Museet (The Nordic Museum) in Stockholm. These were powerful books meant to be handled carefully. After reading up on them a little, it turns out that their purpose was to keep sickness and misfortune at bay. Only a few of these books have survived to present time.

The Black Magic cardigan is decorated with timeless symbols such as crescent moons, full moons, stars and different types of crosses (this type of knitted cross is a common protective symbol on Norwegian lice-pattern cardigans). I hope that the cardigan will become a good companion for you during the dark winter.

YARN: Léttlopi from Ístex, 100% Icelandic wool, 50g (1.8oz) = 100m (109yd)

TENSION: 18 sts × 24 rows in stocking stitch in pattern with needles 5mm = 10 × 10cm (4 × 4in)

SIZES: XS (S) M (L) XL (2XL) 3XL (4XL)

CARDIGAN CHEST WIDTH: 85 (94) 98 (107) 120 (134) 143 (156)cm / 33 ½ (37) 38 ½ (42) 47 ½ (52 ¾ ) 56 ¼ (61 ½)in

CARDIGAN LENGTH: 55 (55.5) 59 (60) 63 (64.5) 66.5 (68)cm / 21 ¾ (21 ¾) 23 ¼ (23 ½) 24 ¾ (25 ½) 26 ¼ (26 ¾)in

CARDIGAN SLEEVE LENGTH: 44 (45) 47 (49) 51 (52) 52 (52)cm / 17 ¼ (17 ¾) 18 ½ (19 ¼) 20 (20 ½) 20 ½ (20 ½)in

AMOUNTS: Colour 1 = 350 (400) 450 (500) 500 (550) 600 (600)g / 12.3 (14.1) 15.9 (17.6) (17.6) 19.4 (21.2) 21.2oz Black Heather (no. 0005), colour 2 = 100 (100) 100 (100) 100 (100) 100 (100)g / 1.8oz Light Ash Heather (no. 0054)

DOUBLE-POINTED NEEDLES: 4.5mm and 5mm

CIRCULAR NEEDLES: 4.5mm and 5mm, 80cm (32in) long

NOTIONS: 9 buttons (18mm in diameter), stitch holder, decorative band (optional)

DIFFICULTY LEVEL: 3 of 3

CONSTRUCTION: Body and sleeves are knit in the round separately and are then placed on the same circular needle. Then the yoke is knit with colourwork pattern, decreases, short rows on the back as well as a neckband. To finish, button bands are added on and the cardigan is cut open (see Knitting School p154). Note that the ribbed sections at the bottom and top are worked back and forth.

TECHNIQUES: M1L = increase 1 st slanting left, see Knitting School, p159.
M1R = increase 1 st slanting right, see Knitting School, p159.
Short rows and wrap and turn: See Knitting School, p158.

## BODY

With 4.5mm circular needle and colour 1, cast on 146 (162) 174 (190) 214 (234) 250 (274) sts.

Work in rib back and forth.

Row 1 (WS): *P2, k2*, repeat from *–* to last 2 sts, p2.

Row 2 (RS): *K2, p2*, repeat from *–* to last 2 sts, k2.

Row 3 (WS): *P2, k2*, repeat from *–* to last 2 sts, p2.

Repeat rows 2 and 3 until the rib measures 5cm (2in). NB: finish the rib with a wrong side row.

Going forward the body is knit in the round in stocking stitch (= knit every row when knitting in the round).

INITIAL ROUND: Change to 5mm needle, and knit and at the same time increase 7 (7) 3 (3) 3 (7) 7 (7) sts evenly spaced over the round = 153 (169) 177 (193) 217 (241) 257 (281) sts.

Then cast on 5 steek stitches using the double twisted loop technique (see video links in the Knitting School on p160). The steek stitches also function as a marker for the beginning and end of a round. (NB: the steek stitches are not included in the cardigan's total stitch count and increases and decreases should not be made within these stitches.)

Continue working in stocking stitch (= knit every round when knitting in the round) until the body measures 25 (26) 27 (28) 29 (30) 31 (32)cm / 9 ¾ (10 ¼) 10 ½ (11) 11 ½ (11 ¾) 12 ¼ (12 ½)in or preferred length. Set the work aside.

## SLEEVES

With 4.5mm dpns and colour 1, cast on 40 (40) 40 (40) 40 (44) 44 (44) sts.

Work in the round in k2, p2 rib stitch for 5cm (2in).

Change to 5mm dpns. Continue working in stocking stitch and at the same time increase 8 (8) 8 (8) 8 (4) 4 (4) sts evenly spaced over the round = 48 (48) 48 (48) 48 (48) 48 (48) sts.

Knit 1 more round.

Knit the colourwork pattern following chart A (stitches 1–6 are repeated a total of 8 times) for 11 rounds.

With colour 1: Work 5 rounds.

INCREASE ROUND: *K1, M1L (see Abbreviations), knit to last st on the round, M1R (see Techniques), k1.

Knit 19 (13) 9 (7) 5 (3) 3 (2) rounds without increases*.

Repeat from *–* a total of 2 (4) 6 (10) 14 (18) 21 (23) times = 52 (56) 60 (68) 76 (84) 90 (94) sts.

Knit until the sleeve measures 44 (45) 47 (49) 51 (52) 52 (52)cm / 17 ¼ (17 ¾) 18 ½ (19 ¼) 20 (20 ½) 20 ½ (20 ½)in or preferred length.

Next round: Knit to last 4 (5) 5 (6) 7 (7) 8 (8) sts on the round.

Transfer the following 8 (10) 10 (12) 14 (14) 16 (16) sts to a stitch holder/length of scrap yarn (= armhole stitches).

Cut the yarn and transfer the sleeve's remaining 44 (46) 50 (56) 62 (70) 74 (78) sts to a stitch holder. Set the work aside and knit another sleeve the same way, but mirror the chart for the other sleeve.

### *Join body and sleeves*

Continue working in the round in stocking stitch.

With 5mm circular needle and colour 1, knit right front's 34 (37) 39 (42) 47 (53) 56 (62) sts. Transfer the following 8 (10) 10 (12) 14 (14) 16 (16) sts to a stitch holder. Knit right sleeve's 44 (46) 50 (56) 62 (70) 74 (78) sts. Knit the back's 69 (75) 79 (85) 95 (107) 113 (125) sts. Transfer the following 8 (10) 10 (12) 14 (14) 16 (16) sts to a stitch holder. Knit left sleeve's 44 (46) 50 (56) 62 (70) 74 (78) sts. Knit left front's 34 (37) 39 (42) 47 (53) 56 (62) sts = 225 (241) 257 (281) 313 (353) 373 (405) sts on the needle. Knit 1 round.

NEXT ROUND, XS, S, M, 2XL: Knit = 225 (241) 257 (353) sts on the needle.

NEXT ROUND, L, XL, 3XL, 4XL: Decrease 8 (8) 4 (4) sts evenly spaced = 273 (305) 369 (401) sts on the needle.

STJÄRNHIMMELN VINTERGATAN

### YOKE

Knit 5 rounds.

Knit the colourwork pattern with decreases and increases following chart B1, rounds 1–46, according to placement below. (Depending on the size the rounds are finished with chart B2 or B3).

XS, M, 2XL: Repeat stitches *1–32* 6 (7) 10 times, then work stitches 1–31 and finally stitches 1–2 in chart B2.

S, L, XL, 3XL, 4XL: Work stitches 25–32, then repeat stitches *1–32* (7) 8 (9) 11 (12) times, then work stitches 1–6 and finally stitches 1–3 in chart B3.

Once the yoke is worked 85 (91) 97 (103) 115 (133) 139 (151) sts remain.

*Back short rows*

With colour 1, now work in stocking stitch back and forth with knit and purl short rows (read about short rows and wrap and turn on p158 in the Knitting School).

Knit 56 (60) 64 (68) 76 (88) 92 (100) sts, wrap and turn. Purl 28 (30) 32 (34) 38 (44) 46 (50) sts, wrap and turn. *Knit to last 4 sts before the turning, wrap and turn. Purl to last 4 sts before the turning, wrap and turn*. Repeat from *–* a total 2 (2) 3 (3) 4 (4) 5 (5) times, then work to end of row and at the same time pick up and work the wrapped stitches.

Work another 1 row where the remaining wrapped stitches are picked up and worked.

### NECKBAND

Knit 1 round and at the same time evenly decrease 3 (1) 3 (1) 1 (11) 13 (21) sts over the round = 82 (90) 94 (102) 114 (122) 126 (130) sts.

Change to 4.5mm circular needle and cast off the 5 steek stitches at the middle of the front.

Work in rib back and forth.

ROW 1 (RS): *K2, p2*, repeat from *–* to last 2 sts, k2.

ROW 2 (WS): *P2, k2*. Repeat from *–* to last 2 sts, p2.

Repeat rows 1 and 2 until the rib measures 4cm (1 ½in). Ending with a WS row.

DECREASE ROW: *K2, p2tog*. Repeat from *–* to last 2 sts, k2 = 62 (68) 71 (77) 86 (92) 95 (98) sts. Cast off loosely in rib.

With 3 5mm dpns, knit together the stitches under the armholes using the 3-needle cast off technique, see Knitting School, p160. Weave in loose ends.

### BUTTON BANDS

*Left button band*

With 4.5mm circular needle and colour 1 (RS), pick up stitches along the left front starting at the top. To ensure the edge has the right amount of stretch you pick up 2 of 3 sts (= *pick up 2 sts, skip the third st*, repeat from *–*). The stitch count must be divisible by 4 + 2.

Now work in rib.

ROW 1 (WS): *P2, k2*, repeat from *–* to last 2 sts, p2.

ROW 2 (RS): *K2, p2*, repeat from *–* to last 2 sts, k2.

ROW 3 (WS): *P2, k2*, repeat from *–* to last 2 sts, p2.

Repeat rows 2 and 3 a total of 4 times (= 9 rows in total). Cast off in rib.

*Right button band*

With 4.5mm circular needle and colour 1 (RS): Pick up stitches along the right front starting at the bottom. Make sure to pick up the same number of stitches as for the left button band. Divide 9 buttonholes (mark with a safety pin) evenly over the button band (each buttonhole goes over 2 sts).

Work in rib as for left button band until row 4.

ROW 4 (buttonhole row 1, RS): Work in established rib until the first buttonhole. Then work as follows: *cast off 2 sts, continue working in established rib until the next buttonhole*, repeat from *–* until all buttonholes have been started and then work in rib to to end of row.

CHART A

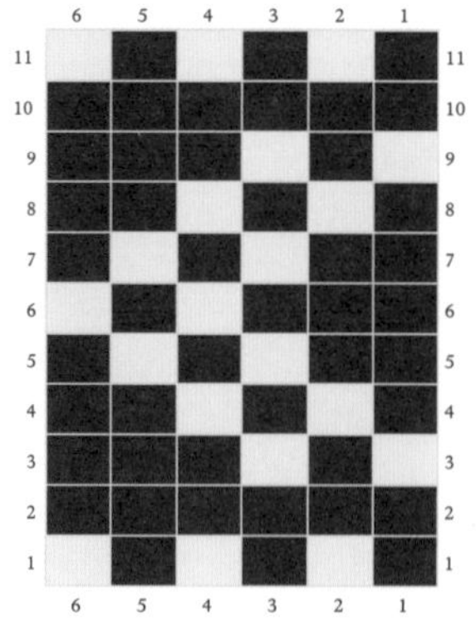

CHART B1

ROW 5 (buttonhole row 2, AS), work in established rib until the first buttonhole and finish as follows: *Cast on 2 sts using the double twisted loop technique, continue working in established rib until next buttonhole*, repeat from *–* until all buttonholes are completed and then work in rib to end of row.

Work another 4 rows in rib and then cast off in rib.

*Cutting the steek*

See Knitting School, p154. Sew a reinforcing seam with sewing thread (by hand using backstitch) on each side of the middle steek stitch. Carefully cut the cardigan open in the middle of the middle steek stitch. (The cut edges will roll in towards the wrong side.)

## FINISHING

Weave in loose ends.

Block the cardigan carefully following the measurements specified and instructions in the Knitting School, p156.

Sew on buttons level with the buttonholes.

Either cover the cut edges on the inside with a decorative band, or fold them in and sew with discreet stitches to the wrong side.

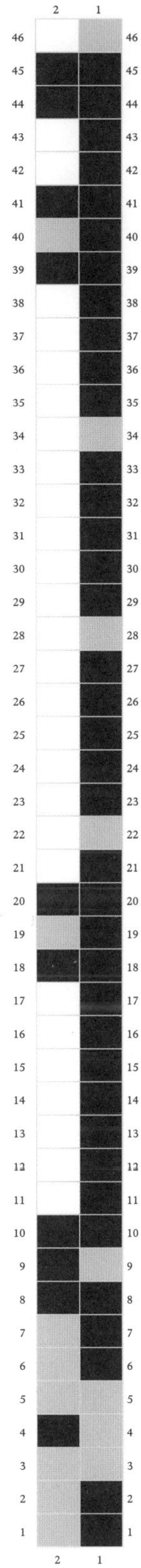

CHART B2

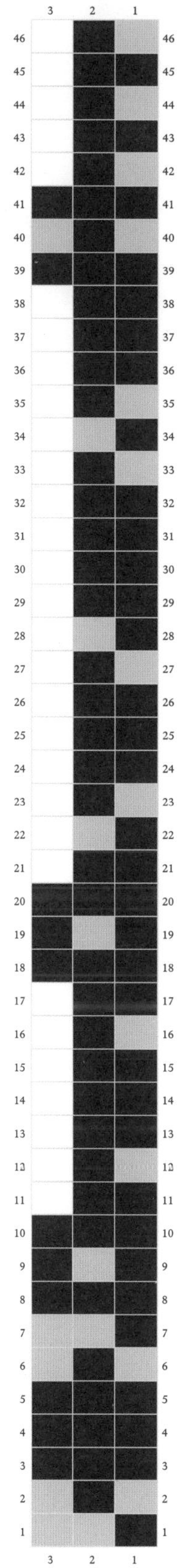

CHART B3

# Sisterhood

My Sisterhood pattern is back – this time in the form of a woolly hat with a pompom. The sisters have once again taken each other's hands and entered the eternal ring dance, where generation after generation help each other forward. The nicest thing about the whirling dance is that there is room for us all in it: sisters, daughters, mothers and grandmothers. We are all an important part of this heart-warming community!

You can match the hat with mittens, socks or cardigan in the same pattern from my previous books.

YARN: Järbo 2 tr ull, 100% wool, 100g (3.5oz) = 300m (328yd)

TENSION: 24 sts × 31 rows in stocking stitch in pattern with needles 3.5mm = 10 × 10 cm (4 × 4in)

SIZES: S (M/L)

HAT CIRCUMFERENCE: 50 (55)cm / 19 ¾ (21 ¾)in

HAT LENGTH: 25 (25)cm / 9 ¾ (9 ¾)

AMOUNTS: Colour 1 = 100g (3.5oz) Blackish (no. 74109), colour 2 = 50g (1.8oz) Natural white (no. 74102)

CIRCULAR NEEDLES: 3.5mm, 40cm (16in) long

DOUBLE-POINTED NEEDLES: 3.5mm

DIFFICULTY LEVEL: 3 of 3

CONSTRUCTION: The hat is knit from the bottom up in colourwork pattern with Latvian braids and a pompom on the top.

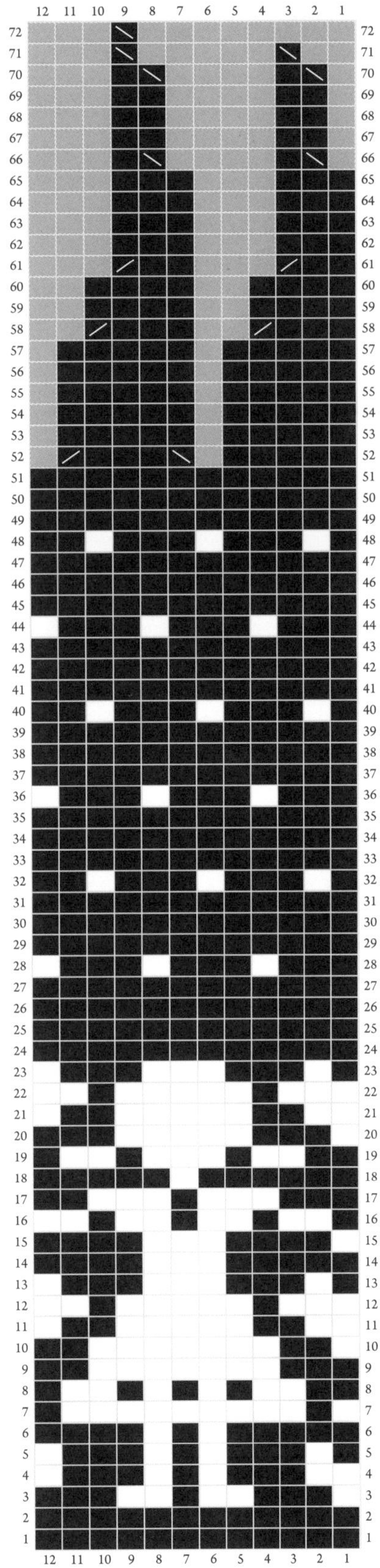

## HAT

*Latvian braid*

See p160 in the Knitting School.

With 3.5mm circular needle and colour 1, cast on 120 (132) sts and start with a Latvian braid.

ROW 1: *K1 with colour 1, k1 with colour 2*, repeat from *–* to last st, k1 with colour 1.

ROW 2: *P1 with colour 1, p1 with colour 2*, repeat from *–* to last st, p1 with colour 1. NB: hold both threads at the front of the work while knitting. At each colour change the new yarn should be brought under the yarn you just knitted with.

ROW 3: *P1 with colour 1, p1 with colour 2*, repeat from *–* to last st, p1 with colour 1. NB: hold both threads at the front of the work while knitting. At each colour change the new yarn should be brought over the yarn you just knitted with.

Change to stocking stitch (= knit all stitches when working in the round).

Knit the pattern following the chart, rounds 1–72 (stitches 1–12 are repeated 10 (11) times per round and decreases are made following the chart). NB: between rounds 25 and 26, a Latvian braid is worked following instructions above.

When the decreases have been made, 10 (11) sts remain.

Cut the yarn, pass it through the remaining stitches and secure.

*Finishing*

Weave in loose ends. Make a yarn pompom, 10–12cm (4–4 ¾in) in diameter, with colour 1 and attach to the top of the hat.

Col. 2

Col. 1

K2tog

SL1 knitwise, k1, pass the slipped stitch over the one you've just knitted

No stitch

ÖSTRA EUROPA
ALLT FÖR ALLAS VÄRLDSATLAS 27

# Tundra

A tundra is a treeless landscape with an Arctic climate. This means that the temperature never gets above ten degrees Celsius. On the tundra, there is always permafrost – meaning that the ground is frozen all year round.

The barren tundra with its creeping plants is the inspiration for this hat and scarf with the same name. Despite the constant cold, there are grasses and lichen that manage to live and thrive in this inhospitable climate. It reminds me how we tackle winter after winter during our lifetime here in the North, often with a stoic patience that is drilled into us from early childhood. We know that the sun will return – even if the winter is long.

The Tundra scarf and hat are designed for those wanting to try out cable knitting. With help from a cable needle the stitches are crossed over to make effectful cables. Knitting cables is not difficult at all. I hope you have the courage to try it out! This set is also good for those who are looking for a quick project in warming wool for the coldest days of the winter.

# Scarf

YARN: Álafosslopi from Ístex, 100% Icelandic wool, 100g (3.5oz) = 100m (106yd)
TENSION: 13 sts × 20 rows in stocking stitch with 7mm needles = 10 × 10cm (4 ×4in)
SIZES: One size
SCARF WIDTH: 27cm / 10 ½in
SCARF LENGTH: 145cm / 57in
AMOUNTS: 300g (10.6oz) Grey Heather (no. 0057)
CIRCULAR NEEDLES: 5mm and 7mm, 40cm (16in) long; straight knitting needles will also work
NOTIONS: 1 cable needle
DIFFICULTY LEVEL: 1 of 3
CONSTRUCTION: The scarf is knit back and forth with ribbed edges on the short sides.

With 5mm circular needle, cast on 42 sts.
(NB: stitch 1 on the right side is always slipped knitwise with the yarn at back of the work and stitch 1 on the wrong side is always slipped purlwise with the yarn in front of the work.)
Work in rib back and forth.
ROW 1 (WS): P2, *k2, p2*, repeat from *–* to end of row.
ROW 2 (RS): K2, *k2, p2*, repeat from *–* to end of row.
ROW 3 (WS): P2, *k2, p2*, repeat from *–* to end of row.
Repeat rows 2 and 3 until the work measures 10cm (4in).
Knit 1 row and at the same time increase 2 sts = 44 sts.
Purl 1 row.
Change to 7mm circular needle.

## WORK THE CABLE PATTERN

ROW 1 (RS): K2, work cable pattern following the chart (see key overleaf), row 1 stitches 1–16 twice, then stitches 1–8 once, then finish with k2.
ROW 2 (WS): P2, work cable pattern following the chart, row 2 stitches 1–16 twice, then stitches 1–8 once, then finish with p2.
ROW 3: K2, work cable pattern according to next row in the chart stitches 1–16 twice, then stitches 1–8 once, then finish with k2.
ROW 4: P2, work cable pattern according to next row in the chart stitches 1–16 twice, then stitches 1–8 once, then finish with p2.
Repeat rows 3–4 until 12 repetitions (1 repetition = rows 1–16) of the chart have been worked. Then continue by working rows 1–8 in the chart the same way as before with side stitches.
Knit 1 row and at the same time decrease 2 sts = 42 sts.
Purl 1 row.
Change to 5mm circular needle and work in rib the same way as in the beginning of the scarf, for 10cm (4in). Finish with a wrong side row.
Cast off in rib.

*Finishing*

Weave in loose ends. Block the scarf carefully following the measurements specified and instructions in the Knitting School, p156.

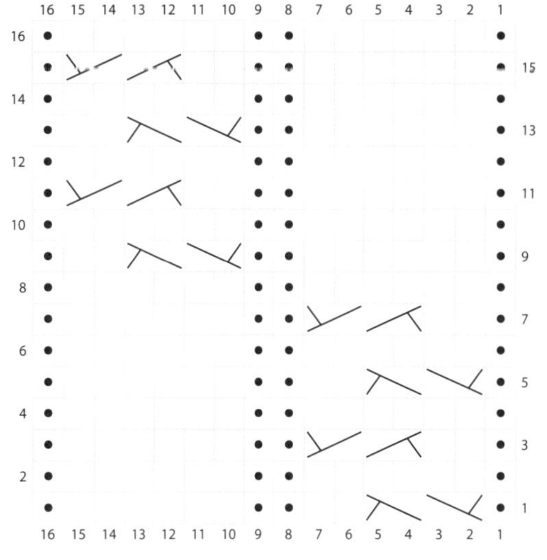

# Hat

YARN: Álafosslopi from Ístex, 100% Icelandic wool, 100g (3.5oz) = 100m (109yd)

TENSION: 13 sts × 20 rows in stocking stitch in pattern with 7mm needles = 10 × 10cm (4 × 4in)

SIZE: One size

HEAD CIRCUMFERENCE: 53–55cm (20 ¾–21 ¾in)

HAT CIRCUMFERENCE: 46cm (18in) (unstretched)

HAT LENGTH: 24cm (9 ½in)

AMOUNTS: 100g (3.5oz) Grey Heather (no. 0057)

CIRCULAR NEEDLES: 5mm and 7mm, 40cm (16in) long

NOTIONS: 1 cable needle, 1 stitch marker

DIFFICULTY LEVEL: 1 of 3

CONSTRUCTION: The hat is knit from the bottom up with a ribbed edge.

With 5mm circular needle, cast on 72 sts and work in the round in k2, p2 rib stitch until the work measures 10cm (4in) (NB: place 1 stitch marker at the beginning of the round to make it easier to see when you have completed a round).

Change to 7mm circular needle.

Knit 1 round and at the same time increase 8 sts evenly spaced over the round = 80 sts.

Work cable pattern following the chart, rows 1–16, using a cable needle, stitches 1–16 are repeated 5 times for every round.

Knit 1 round and at the same time decrease 8 sts evenly spaced over the round = 72 sts.

## DECREASE FOR TOP OF HAT

ROUND 1: *K2, k2tog*, repeat from *–* to end of round = 54 sts.

ROUNDS 2 AND 3: Knit.

ROUND 4: *K4, k2tog*, repeat from *–* to end or round = 45 sts.

ROUND 5: *K2tog, k2tog, k1*. Repeat from *–* to end or round = 27 sts.

ROUND 6: *K2tog, k1*, repeat from *–* to end of round = 18 sts.

ROUND 7: *K2tog*, repeat from *–* to end of round = 9 sts.

Cut the yarn, pass through the remaining stitches and secure.

## FINISHING

Weave in loose ends. Block the hat carefully following the measurements specified and instructions in the Knitting School, p156.

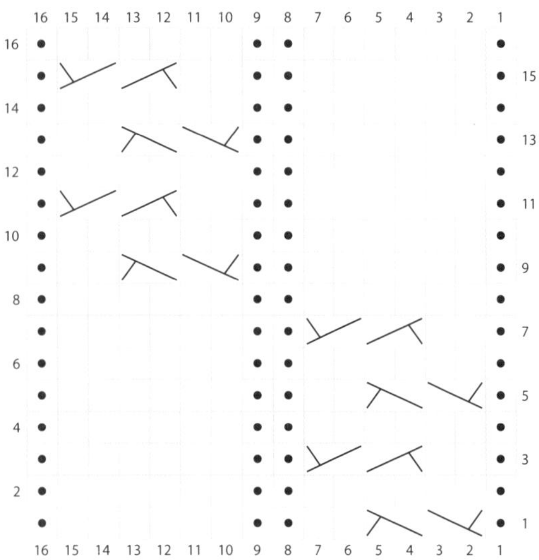


= Knit on right side, purl on wrong side

• = Purl on right side, knit on wrong side

= Place 2 sts on a cable needle at the back of the work, k2, then knit the 2 sts on the cable needle

= Place 2 sts on a cable needle at the front of the work, k2, then knit the 2 sts on the cable needle

# January

January is the first month of the year – a time for glimmering hope, a new start and new paths. These are the reasons why I love New Year's Day. How it spreads out before me, like a blank slate ready to be filled with sparkling colours. I usually spend that day in the softest possible way: on a sofa, with the sounds from the New Year's Concert from Vienna on in the background. The smell of blossoming hyacinths fills the air and, of course, this is the time to cast on a new knitting project too. Are you new to knitting and want to start the year by acquiring a new skill? If so, I warmly recommend this beginner jumper – a jumper version of the Prima cardigan that you'll find in my book *Cardigans*.

YARN: Børstet Alpakka from Sandnes, 96% brushed alpaca, 4% nylon, 50g (1.8oz) = 110m (328yd)

TENSION: 12 sts × 20 rows in stocking stitch using 8mm needles = 10 × 10cm (4 × 4in)

SIZES: XS (S) M (L) XL/2XL (3XL/4XL)

JUMPER CHEST WIDTH: 100 (116) 132 (146) 160 (176)cm / 39 ½ (45 ¾) 52 (57 ½) 63 (69 ¼)in

POSITIVE EASE: 20–40cm (7 ¾–15 ¾in)

JUMPER LENGTH: 52 (52) 54 (56) 58 (58)cm / 20 ½ (20 ½) 21 ¼ (22) 22 ¾ (22 ¾)in

JUMPER SLEEVE LENGTH: 49 (49) 49 (50) 50 (50)cm / 19 ½ (19 ½) 19 ½ (19 ¾) 19 ¾ (19 ¾)in

AMOUNTS: 250 (300) 300 (350) 350 (400)g Natur Tweed (no. 2523)

CIRCULAR NEEDLES: 7mm and 8mm, 80cm (32in) long

DOUBLE-POINTED NEEDLES: 7mm and 8mm

NOTIONS: Stitch holder

DIFFICULTY LEVEL: 1 of 3

CONSTRUCTION: January is a seamless jumper that is knit from the top down. First the upper part of the back is knit, then stitches are picked up for the fronts – directly from the back. Then the body is knitted into one piece and is finished on a circular needle. To finish, the sleeves are knit on. Note that the jumper is oversize. Add 20–40cm (7 ¾–15 ¾in) for the chest width when choosing size.

TECHNIQUES: M1R = increase 1 st slanting right, see Knitting School, p159.

M1L = increase 1 st slanting left, see Knitting School, p159.

## BACK

With 8mm circular needle, cast on 61 (71) 81 (89) 97 (107) sts.

ROW 1 (WS): Purl.

ROW 2 (RS): Knit.

ROW 3 (WS): Purl.

Repeat rows 2 and 3 until the work measures 25 (25) 25 (27) 27 (27)cm / 9 ¾ (9 ¾) 9 ¾ (10 ½) 10 ½ (10 ½)in. NB: finish with a wrong side row. Set the stitches aside on a stitch holder/length of scrap yarn.

### *Left front*

Now, pick up left front's stitches from the back's cast-on edge.

With 8mm circular needle, hold the back with the right side facing you. Pick up 20 (25) 30 (34) 38 (43) sts in the 20 (25) 30 (34) 38 (43) sts to the left on the back's cast-on edge.

ROW 1 (WS): Purl.

ROW 2 (RS): K1, M1R (see Techniques), knit to end of row.

Repeat rows 1 and 2 until you have 27 (32) 37 (41) 45 (50) sts on the needle

Then repeat row once more.

Cut the yarn and set the stitches aside on a stitch holder.

### *Right front*

Now the right front's stitches are picked up in the back's cast-on edge.

With 8mm circular needle, hold the back with the right side facing you and start at the right end. Pick up 20 (25) 30 (34) 38 (43) new stitches in the back's cast-on edge.

ROW 1 (WS): Purl.

ROW 2 (RS): Knit to last 1 sts on the row, M1L (see Abbreviations), k1. Repeat rows 1 and 2 until you have 27 (32) 37 (41) 45 (50) sts on the needle.

Then repeat row 1 another 1 time.

ROW 3: Knit to end of row, cast on 7 (7) 7 (7) 7 (7) new stitches using the twisted loop technique (see video links in the Knitting School, p160).

Then knit the stitches set aside from the left front = 61 (71) 81 (89) 97 (107) sts.

ROW 4: Purl.

ROW 5: Knit.

Repeat rows 4 and 5 until the front measures 25 (25) 25 (27) 27 (27)cm / 9 ¾ (9 ¾) 9 ¾ (10 ½) 10 ½ (10 ½)in. NB: finish with a wrong side row. Set the stitches aside on a stitch holder.

## BODY

Now the front and back are knit together.

With 8mm circular needle, knit across the back's 61 (71) 81 (89) 97 (107) sts (going forward the round begins here) together with the front's 61 (71) 81 (89) 97 (107) sts = 122 (142) 162 (178) 194 (214) sts on the needle.

ROUND 1: Knit across all stitches starting with the front's stitches.

Repeat round 1 until the body measures 23 (23) 25 (25) 27 (27)cm / 9 (9) 9 ¾ (9 ¾) 10 ¾ (10 ¾)in from the armhole.

Change to 7mm circular needle and work in k1, p1 rib for 7cm (2 ¾in). Cast off loosely in rib.

## SLEEVES

With 8mm dpns: Pick up 60 (60) 60 (66) 66 (66)sts around the whole armhole starting at the bottom of the armhole.

Knit in the round until the sleeve measures 25cm (9 ¾in).

DECREASE ROUND: K1, SL1, k1 and pass the slipped st over the one you've just knitted, knit to last 3 sts, k2tog, k1 = 2 sts decreased.

Knit one round. Continue to make decreases following instructions for decrease round every other round until you have 28 (28) 28 (30) 30 (30) sts on the needles.

With 7mm dpns, work in the round in k1, p1 rib for 7cm (2 ¾in).

Cast off loosely in rib.

Knit one more sleeve the same way.

## NECKBAND

With 7mm dpns, pick up 56 sts evenly spaced over the neckband.

Work in the round in k1, p1 rib for 3 rounds.

Cast off loosely in rib.

## FINISHING

Weave in loose ends. Block the jumper carefully following the measurements specified and instructions in the Knitting School, p156.

# Wolf Winter

In the past, if the weather was severely cold, packs of wolves would close in on houses and domestic animals in the search for food. Thus, the expression wolf winter means an extremely cold winter. It is also likely to be connected to Old Norse mythology, where they spoke of a Fimbulwinter that would precede the end of the world. The Fimbulwinter would arrive when Fenrir, the wolf of wolves, devoured the sun. Read more about it on p47, where you'll find the Fimbul scarf.

The Wolf Winter mittens are adorned with a snowflake and they warm well thanks to the thick Icelandic yarn and the two-colour pattern.

YARN: Álafosslopi from Ístex, 100% Icelandic wool, 100g (3.5oz) = 100m (109yd)

TENSION: 17 sts × 18 rows stocking stitch in pattern with 5mm needles = 10 × 10cm (4 × 4in)

SIZES: One size

MITTEN WIDTH: 10.5cm (4 ¼in)

MITTEN LENGTH: 26cm (10 ¼in)

AMOUNTS: Colour 1 = 70g (2.5oz) Light Beige Heather (no. 0086), colour 2 = 30g (1oz) White (no. 0051)

DOUBLE-POINTED NEEDLES: 4.5mm and 5mm

DIFFICULTY LEVEL: 2 of 3

CONSTRUCTION: The mittens are knit from the cuff up with a traditional afterthought thumb.

## RIGHT MITTEN

### *Cuff*

With 4.5mm dpns and colour 1, cast on 32 sts and divide them evenly over four needles (8 sts on each needle).

WORK IN THE ROUND IN RIB STITCH: *K1, p1*, repeat from *–* to end of round. Repeat until the cuff measures 6cm (2 ¼in).

### *Hand*

Change to 5mm dpns.

Knit 1 round and increase 4 sts evenly spaced over the round = 36 sts.

Knit 1 round. Work in stocking stitch going forward (= knit all rounds).

Knit the pattern following the chart, stitches 1–11 (repeat stitches 1–18, 2 times per round).

### *Prepare for thumb*

Knit the pattern following the chart (round 12) for the round's initial 18 stitches. Then take a length of yarn in a contrasting colour and knit the following 7 sts with it. Transfer these 7 sts back to the left needle and knit them again following the chart. Knit the round's remaining 11 sts following the chart.

### *Continue the hand*

Knit the pattern following the chart, stitches 13–29, and then continue with colour 1 for another 3 rounds.

DECREASE ROUNDS FOR TOP OF MITTEN: SL1, k1 and pass the slipped st over the one you've just knitted, knit to last 3 sts on needle 2: K2tog, k1. Needle 3: SL1, k1 and pass the slipped st over the one you've just knitted. Knit to last 3 sts on needle 4: K2tog, k1 = 4 sts decreased.

Repeat the decrease round every round until 8 sts remain. Cut the yarn and pass through the remaining stitches. Weave in loose ends.

## THUMB

Remove the thread that marks the thumb.

With four 5mm dpns and colour 1, pick up the 14 thumb stitches and work in the round until the thumb measures 6cm (2 ¼in).

DECREASE ROUND: *K2tog*, repeat from *–* to end of round = 7 sts.

Cut the yarn, pass the thread through the remaining stitches and pull tight. Weave in loose ends.

## LEFT MITTEN

Knit as for the right mitten, but mirror the pattern by knitting the chart from left to right, instead of from right to left.

Prepare for the thumb by knitting pattern following the chart: First 29 sts, then knit the following 7 sts with a length of yarn in a contrasting colour. Transfer these 7 sts to the left needle and knit them following the chart.

DECREASE ROUND FOR TOP OF MITTEN: K1, SL1, k1 and pass the slipped st over the one you've just knitted, knit to last 2 sts on needle 2: k2tog. Needle 3: K1, SL1, k1 and pass the slipped st over the one you've just knitted, knit to last 2 sts on needle 4: K2tog = 4 sts decreased.

# Love

The great, the wild – the patient and the life-long. The everyday and the platonic. The unrequited and the misunderstood. The courageous and the self-sacrificing. The first. All these types of love we get to celebrate on Valentine's Day, the 14th February – in Sweden known as All Hearts' Day. The day has been associated with romance and love as far back as medieval times, when the tradition of celebrating one's sweetheart – Valentin – took off in England, Scotland and France.

The Love jumper is knitted in rib all the way through, which makes it soft and comfortable. Because it's knitted with two strands of yarn (one merino wool and one mohair silk), it's also warm and fluffy. Almost like a hug full of love.

YARN: Double Sunday, 100% merino wool, 50g (1.8oz) = 108m (118yd), and Tynn Silk Mohair, 57% mohair, 28% silk and 15% wool, 25g (0.9oz) = 212m (232yd)

TENSION: 26 sts × 26 rows in rib stitch with 4mm needles = 10 × 10cm (4 × 4in)

SIZES: XS/S (M) L (XL) 2XL (3XL)

JUMPER CHEST WIDTH: 96 (104) 112 (120) 132 (144)cm / 37 ¾ (41) 44 (47 ¼) 52 (56 ¾)in

JUMPER LENGTH: 47 (49) 51 (53) 54 (56)cm / 18 ½ (19 ¼) 20 (20 ¾) 21 ¼ (22)in

JUMPER SLEEVE LENGTH: 49 (50) 51 (52) 52 (53)cm / 19 ¼ (19 ¾) 20 (20 ½) 20 ½ (20 ¾)in

AMOUNTS: Colour 1 = 500 (550) 600 (650) 700 (750)g / 17.6 (19.4) 21.2 (22.9) 24.7 (26.5)oz Double Sunday, Jazzy Pink (no. 4600), colour 2: 125 (150) 150 (175) 175 (200)g / 4.4 (5.3) 5.3 (6.2) 6.2 (7.1)oz Tynn Silk Mohair, Jazzy Pink, (no. 4600)

CIRCULAR NEEDLES: 4mm, 40 and 80cm (16 and 32in) long

DOUBLE-POINTED NEEDLES: 4mm

NOTIONS: 2 stitch markers

DIFFICULTY LEVEL: 2 of 3

CONSTRUCTION: The jumper is knit from the bottom up with two different yarns held together. First the body is knit in the round in one piece, then the back and front are knit separately, back and forth in rows. The sleeves are knit in the round, the sleeve caps are shaped by knitting back and forth. After the parts have been assembled, the neckband is knit in the round.

## BODY

With 4mm circular needle and two strands of yarn, cast on 248 (272) 288 (312) 344 (376) sts.

Place a stitch marker to mark the beginning of the round. Work in the round in k2, p2 rib. Continue to work in rib until the work measures 24 (25) 26 (27) 28 (29)cm / 9 ½ (9 ¾) 10 ¼ (10 ½) 11 (11 ½)in

Now a new beginning of the round is marked by knitting the first stitch on the round then moving the first stitch marker there = new beginning of round. The round will start with k1, p2. Also mark the middle of the row after 124 (136) 144 (156) 172 (188) sts with a second stitch marker.

*Divide for front and back*

Work in rib to last 2 (4) 6 (10) 12 (14) sts before the second marker.

Cast off the following 4 (8) 12 (20) 24 (28) sts for the armhole.

Work in rib to last 2 (4) 6 (10) 12 (14) sts before the first marker (beginning of round).

Cast off 2 (4) 6 (10) 12 (14) sts at the end of the round and another 2 (4) 6 (10) 12 (14) sts at the beginning of next round. Now both the front and back are made up of 120 (128) 132 (136) 148 (160) sts.

Set the stitches for the front aside.

## BACK

Now make decreases for the armholes at the same time as you continue to work in rib. NB: going forward the 3 stitches at each end are always worked in stocking stitch (= knit on the right side and purl on the wrong side).

DECREASE ROW: K2, SL1 knitwise, SL1 knitwise, transfer both slipped stitches back onto the left needle and knit together through the back loop. Knit in established rib to last 4 sts on the row, k2tog, k2 = 2 sts decreased.

Repeat the decreases another 7 times every other row = 104 (112) 116 (120) 132 (144) sts.

Work in established pattern until the armhole measures 19 (20) 21 (22) 22 (23)cm / 7 ½ (7 ¾) 8 ¼ (8 ¾) 8 ¾ (9)in from the division.

Cast off for shoulders on both sides every other row:

XS/S: [6 sts] 3 times and [7 sts] 2 times
M: [7 sts] 4 times and [8 sts] 1 time
L: [7 sts] 4 times and [8 sts] 1 time
XL: [8 sts] 5 times
2XL: [9 sts] 4 times and [8 sts] 1 time
3XL: [8 sts] 6 times

Set 40 (40) 44 (40) 44 (48) sts aside.

## FRONT

Knit the same way as the back, but start shape for the neckline when the armhole measures 14 (15) 16 (17) 17 (18)cm / 5 ½ (6) 6 ¼ (6 ¾) 6 ¾ (7)in. Transfer the 32 (32) 28 (32) 28 (32) sts in the middle onto a thread and knit the right of the neckline first.

Next row is worked from the right side to last 3 sts before the neckline, k2tog k1 = 1 st decreased. Continue to decrease 1 st at the neckline every other row another 3 (3) 7 (3) 7 (7) times. The first 3 stitches on the row from the wrong side are always purled.

NB: when the work measures 19 (20) 21 (22) 22 (23)cm / 7 ½ (7 ¾) 8 ¼ (8 ¾) 8 ¾ (9)in, cast off for shoulder on the right-hand side every other row:

XS/S: [6 sts] 3 times and [7 sts] 2 times
M: [7 sts] 4 times and [8 sts] 1 time
L: [7 sts] 4 times and [8 sts] 1 time
XL: [8 sts] 5 times
2XL: [9 sts] 4 times and [8 sts] 1 time
3XL: [8 sts] 6 times

Knit the left of the neckline the same way but make the decreases for the neckline as follows: K1, SL1 knitwise, SL1 knitwise, transfer both slipped stitches back onto the left needle and knit together through the back loop.

Set the 32 (32) 28 (32) 28 (32) sts for the neckband aside.

### SLEEVES

With 4mm dpns and two strands of yarn, cast on 64 (68) 68 (72) 72 (72) sts and work in the round in k2, p2 rib. Place 1 marker at the beginning of the round.

Work until the sleeve measures 7 (8) 11 (12) 12 (13)cm / 2 ¾ (3 ¼) 4 ¼ (4 ¾) 4 ¾ (5)in. Now a new beginning of the round is marked by knitting the first stitch on the round, then moving the first stitch marker there = new beginning of round. The round will start with k1, p2. Now increases are made on each side of the beginning of round.

INCREASE ROUND: K1, increase 1 st in established rib pattern, work in rib to last st on the round, increase 1 st in established rib pattern, k1.

Repeat the increases every 3.5 (3.5) 2.5 (2.5) 2.5 (2)cm / 1 ½ (1 ½) 1 (1) 1 (¾)in, 11 (11) 15 (15) 15 (19) times = 88 (92) 100 (104) 104 (112) sts.

Knit until the work measures 49 (50) 51 (52) 52 (53)cm / 19 ¼ (19 ¾) 20 (20 ½) 20 ½ (20 ¾)in.

NEXT ROUND: Knit until 4 (4) 6 (8) 10 (12) sts remain before the beginning of the next round, cast off 4 (4) 6 (8) 10 (12) sts and another 4 (4) 6 (8) 10 (12) sts at the beginning of the following round.

### SHAPING THE SLEEVE CAP

Work in rib back and forth with 3 sts stocking stitch in both sides and the armholes.

DECREASE ROW: K2, SL1 knitwise, SL1 knitwise, transfer both slipped stitches back to the left needle and knit together through the back loop. Knit in established rib to last 4 sts on the row, k2tog, k2 = 2 sts decreased.

Repeat decreases another 7 times on every other row and then 8 times on every row. Then cast off another [2 sts] 1 time, [3 (3) 4 (4) 3 (4) sts] 1 time, and [4 (4) 5 (5) 4 (5) sts] 1 time on both sides every other row. Cast off remaining sts.

Knit one more sleeve the same way.

### FINISHING

Block the parts carefully following instructions in the Knitting School, p156.

Sew together the shoulder seams. Sew the sleeves to the armholes. Weave in loose ends.

### NECKBAND

With 4 mm circular needle, pick up the stitches that were set aside for the neckband and stitches from both sides of the held stitches so that the rib pattern can continue. Pick up the held stitches at the neckline and stitches on both sides of the held stitches so that the rib pattern can continue unbroken at the centre front and centre back. Work in the round in rib stitch until the neckband measures 10cm (4in).

Cast off in rib.

# Knitting School

### SIZE AND POSITIVE EASE, JUMPERS AND CARDIGANS

The positive ease of a garment means how spacious it is, that is, how it will fit. When you choose a size, you first need to think about what fit you would prefer and then add a few of centimetres to your bust measurements.

Here's how to calculate:

TIGHT FIT = add 0–5cm/0–2in positive ease
NORMAL FIT = add 5–15cm/2–6in positive ease
OVERSIZED FIt = add 20–40cm/8–16in positive ease

This means that if you want a cardigan with a normal fit, and you measure 100cm/39½in around your bust, you should knit a cardigan that has a bust measurement of around 110cm/43½in. This will give you a positive ease of 10cm/4in. Therefore, you should choose the size that is closest to 110cm/43½in.

Note that most of the patterns in this book are constructed with a normal fit in mind. If a garment is designed to be tight or oversized, the pattern will make this clear.

### KNITTING A CARDIGAN IN THE ROUND

In the Nordic countries cardigans have traditionally been knitted in the round to make colourwork easier, since stocking stitch is only made up of knit stitches when knitting in the round. This way you don't need to knit colourwork with purl stitches, which is more time consuming.

When a cardigan is knitted in the round it is cut open afterwards, to make an opening. The cut is made in the middle of a number of 'steek stitches' which are cast on in addition to the original number of stitches. This section is called the 'steek'. You could say that the steek forms a 'bridge' between the front pieces.

Techniques for cutting the steek are described in this chapter. What can be reassuring to know is that the stitches hold together very well, thanks to the wool fibres' ability to hook onto each other. Because of this there is no risk that your knitting will unravel when cutting – as long as you follow the instructions below. But keep in mind that more slippery yarns, such as cotton and acrylics, don't have the same ability to hold together, in case you choose different yarns than those that have been specified in this book.

### SEWING REINFORCING SEAMS

I always sew my reinforcing seams by hand using backstitch, standard sewing thread and a sewing needle. This way I keep in control over the knitted material and can therefore avoid pulling or puckering the structure. In sewing by hand, I get a flexible and correctly placed seam in an easy and practical way.

Sew one reinforcing seam on each side of the middle stitch, two reinforcing seams altogether.

### CUTTING THE STEEK

When the reinforcing seams are in place it's time to cut the cardigan open. Place the cardigan on a level surface where you have a lot of room to manoeuvre. Use a small, sharp pair of craft scissors when cutting. Work slowly and methodically when you cut so that you are in control of what you're doing. Let the left hand (or the right hand if you are left handed) follow and support where you cut, so that the front panels are separated from the back panel. Then you don't run the risk of cutting into the back panel by mistake.

Cut the steek open by following the line in the middle of the middle stitch. Tip: if you want to separate the front panels and the back panel completely when you cut you can pull the cardigan over an ironing board (pull it over from the bottom opening, so that the bottom hem ends up around the middle of the ironing board and the neckline towards the end where the ironing board narrows). This way you will get a level surface to work on.

### MOUNTING THE CUT EDGES

The cut edges will roll towards the inside once the steek has been cut, and can be sewn down against the inside with yarn, darning needle and small, discreet whip stitches. Or you can cover the cut edges by sewing on a decorative band.

### COVERING THE CUT EDGES WITH A BAND

Covering the cut edges on a cardigan with a decorative band is a nice finish that adds extra strength to the front edges.

You need 1–2m (1–2yd) of band depending on the length of the cardigan, and I recommend that you choose a band that is at least 1.5cm (½in) wide. It's important that both edges remain evenly long, meaning that none of the edges are stretched out more than the other when the band is sewn on. Therefore, the band should be cut into two equal lengths before you do anything else.

Measure the length on one of the cut edges when stretched out to a good length. Then add 2cm (¾in) seam allowance at each end for a total of 4cm (1 ½in). Pin both bands to the inside of the cardigan so that they cover the cut edges and fold in the edges at each end. Make sure the cut edges are stretched evenly underneath the bands. Then sew the edges of the bands in place with sewing thread using small and discreet stitches.

### AVOIDING HOLES ON SLEEVES AND THUMBS

When you knit on sleeves and come to the transition between the new stitches and the stitches that have been put on hold from the yoke, there is a risk that a hole appears at the place of the transition. I usually solve it by picking up a stitch in one of the loops right at the point of the transition and placing it on the left needle, and then knit it together with the first of the stitches that was put on hold. Then knit the rest of the held stitches.

Avoid a hole at the next transition by picking up a stitch in one of the loops at the transition, as well as an ordinary stitch of the ones that are being picked up. Place these two stitches on the left needle and knit them together. Then continue picking up the remaining new stitches.

Using the same technique, you can avoid holes by knitting half of the stitches for the thumb, picking up one of the loops in the 'gap' and place it on the left needle. Knit the picked-up loop together with the round's starting stitch.

# Finishing

## BLOCKING A GARMENT

1. Fill a sink, tub or bucket with tepid water.
2. Add a dash of wool detergent (there are various brands on the market, with or without fragrance, and most of them have a slightly softening quality).
3. Soak the garment carefully. Don't rub or stretch, just let the water soak through the garment gradually by turning and moving the garment around in the water.
4. Then rinse the garment 2–3 times in water without anything added. In this step the water should also be tepid, that is, the same temperature as before.

## DRYING AND SHAPING

1. Take the garment out of the water, gently squeeze out water and spread it out on a dry and clean terry towel. Squeeze out the water by rolling up the towel and cardigan to a hard roll. Place the roll on the floor and step on it to squeeze out as much water as possible.
2. Spread the garment out on a level, clean and dry surface – for example a dry terry towel, a rug or a blocking mat.
3. Shape the garment so that it is lying flat without any folds or creases, and so that the proportions look good. This step is easiest if you have a blocking mat, since the coarse surface means it's easy to get the cardigan to stay in its required place. On a blocking mat you can also pin specific parts in their right position, by using special stainless steel blocking pins. You should avoid stretching the garment too much (and rib shouldn't be stretched at all), but if necessary you can carefully try to widen or lengthen parts of a cardigan that have ended up with slightly wrong proportions – for example a button edge that is slightly shorter than the actual cardigan, or a sleeve that seems narrower than the other sleeve. It's good to take your time on this step so that you shape the garment carefully with your hands, making it as straight and smooth as possible.
4. Then let the cardigan dry flat, preferably in a warm place, until completely dry. Repeat this process when your garment needs washing again.

## CHOOSING BUTTONS

Buttons are an important and beautiful detail on your cardigan. They come in many different materials: mother of pearl, wood, leather, porcelain, metal and plastic. I prefer buttons made from a natural material, such as wood or mother of pearl (particularly antique ones of good quality). These materials go so well together with wool and age beautifully from use. At the same time it can be fun to use plastic, glass or porcelain if you want to match a specific colour in the cardigan's pattern.

## SEWING ON BUTTONS

I always sew on buttons using doubled sewing thread. My friend Kerstin taught me this, making it twice as fast.

Method: Thread the needle, pass the thread through so that the needle ends up at the middle of the thread's length. Tie a knot at the end and then sew the button on.

## MENDING RIB CUFFS

You can knit new rib cuffs if the old ones get too worn down. Not just for cardigans and jumpers, but also for mittens and socks.

Method: Divide/place the stitches of the cuff onto four dpns by threading on every other loop onto the needles. This is done at a point where the structure is still intact. Cut off the worn-down section but leave around 1cm (½in) of knitted rib next to the needles.

Using the same or a similar yarn to what was used for the garment, knit new rib to length of your choice. Cast off in rib. Unravel the remaining part of the old cuff and weave in loose ends on the inside.

### MAKE MENDING YOUR GARMENTS EASIER

It's nice to add an extra button to the inside of a cardigan, so that it's there as a spare in case one of the cardigan's buttons drops off and gets lost. You can also wind some 'darning yarn' onto one of the leftover yarn ball bands, and keep this in a folder. This makes it easy to find the right yarn when the garment needs mending, increasing the longevity of your garment.

# Techniques featured in the book

### COLOURWORK

Knitting patterns using two or several colours at the same time is a common technique in Swedish and Nordic knitting traditions. The technique gives a dense and warming structure since you end up with double or triple strands of yarn as you knit.

There are different ways of holding the yarn when you knit colourwork. In Sweden it's common to hold the yarn in your left hand: one thread over the index finger and one over the middle finger, then you gather the threads in the hand and hold them together with your ring finger and little finger. But there are other ways of holding the yarn – I hold one thread over my thumb and one over my index finger, for example. Try and see what works the best for you! The most important thing is that you keep an even tension in both threads, so that the yarn that is on hold for the moment doesn't pull at the wrong side.

When you knit a pattern using two colours, you usually regard one colour as the dominant colour (the highlight) and the other as the background. You should hold the yarn so that the dominant colour sits closest to the work and the yarn is always carried under. This way these stitches will become dominant and be more visible than the background. The background colour should instead sit furthest away from the work and always be carried over. It's important to be consistent with the order of the colours, otherwise the pattern will become unclear.

When knitting with one colour, the other will run along at the wrong side. The thread at the wrong side should have the same tension as the rest of the work, otherwise the knitting will get bumpy (if you pull it too tight) or shapeless (if you don't pull it enough). If you knit more than 3–4 consecutive stitches in the same colour it can be a good idea to catch the yarn that runs along the wrong side by wrapping the yarn you're knitting with around it. This way you avoid long 'floats', threads that catch easily when you put on or take off a garment. Just make sure not to catch the yarn at the same place on several consecutive rounds; instead change the placement for each round – otherwise the thread at the back can become visible through the knitting.

To get a successful end result when knitting colourwork, it's important that you:

- Keep your tension as even as possible.
- Keep a good tension on the thread that runs at the wrong side.
- Hold the pattern colour and the background colour in the same order every round.
- Catch the yarn when knitting more than 3–4 consecutive stitches in the same colour.
- Don't catch the yarn at the same place on several consecutive rounds.

### SHAPING A RAISED SECTION, SHORT ROWS

To get a good fit, a raised section using short rows is knitted onto several of the seamless cardigans/jumpers, some of the sock heels and the hotpants.

### WRAP AND TURN

ON THE RIGHT SIDE: Place the thread at the front of the work, slip next stitch moving it to the right needle. Place the thread at the back of the work and then move the slipped stitch back to the left needle. Turn. The thread is now wrapped around the stitch.

ON THE WRONG SIDE: Place the thread at the back of the work, slip the next stitch moving it to the right needle. Place the thread at the front of the work and move the stitch back to the left needle. Turn. The thread is now wrapped around the stitch.

WORKING A WRAPPED STITCH: When you work a wrapped stitch you go through both the stitch itself and the wrapped thread at the same time – knit on the right side and purl on the wrong side.

### STITCH AND SLIP MARKERS

Stitch markers are practical little tools made from plastic or metal, for example, that are placed on the needle between two stitches. In this book, stitch markers are used regularly to mark where the raglan seams are placed. 'Slip marker' means that you slip the marker from the left needle to the right. NB: you can easily make your own stitch markers from tied yarn ends.

### ABBREVIATIONS

K = knit
M1B = increase 1 st in the stitch below
M1L = increase 1 st slanting left
M1R = increase 1 st slanting right
PM = place marker
P = purl
RS = right side
SM = slip marker
SS = stocking stitch
ST/S = stitch/es
TOG = together
WS = wrong side
YO = yarn over

### DECREASES

DECREASE SLANTING RIGHT: Knit 2 stitches together (k2tog) = 1 stitch decreased.

DECREASE SLANTING LEFT: Slip 1 stitch, knit 1 and pass the slipped stitch over the knitted stitch = 1 stitch decreased.

## INCREASES, THREE VARIATIONS

*Increase slanting left (M1L)*

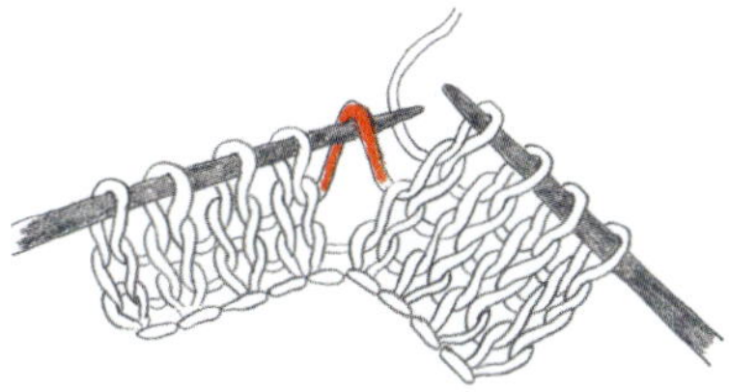

1. Pick up the thread in between the stitches, from the front with the left needle, to form a new stitch.

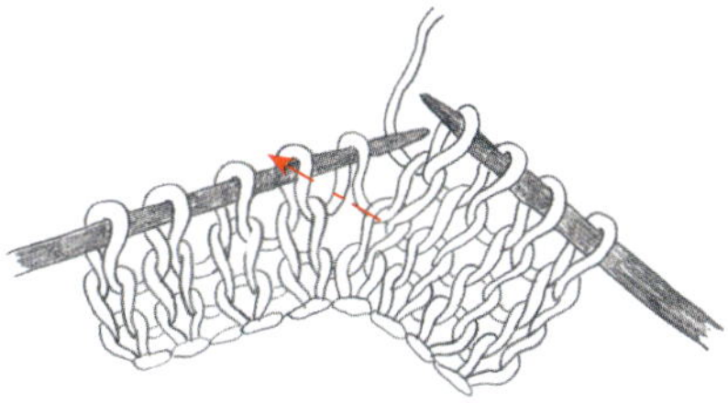

2. Knit 1 stitch through the back loop, as shown by the arrow.

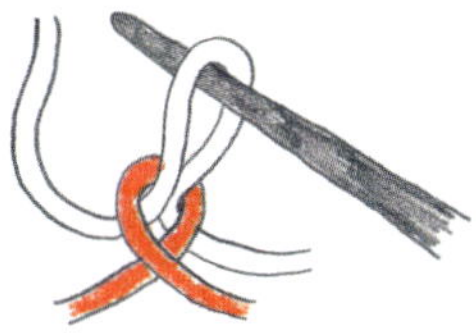

3. A new stitch slanting left has been made.

*Increase slanting right (M1R)*

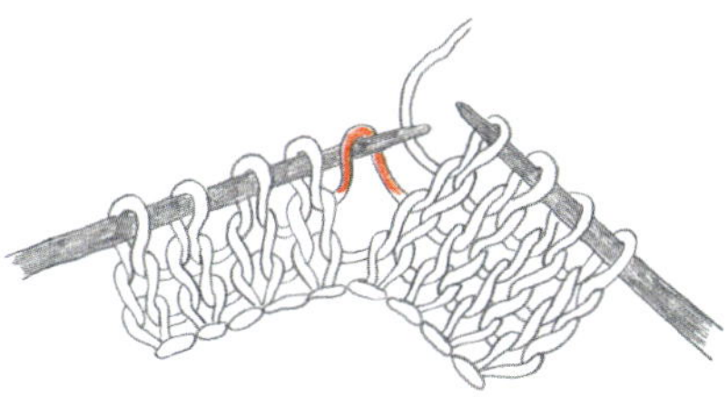

1. Pick up the thread in between the stitches, from behind with left needle, to form a new stitch.

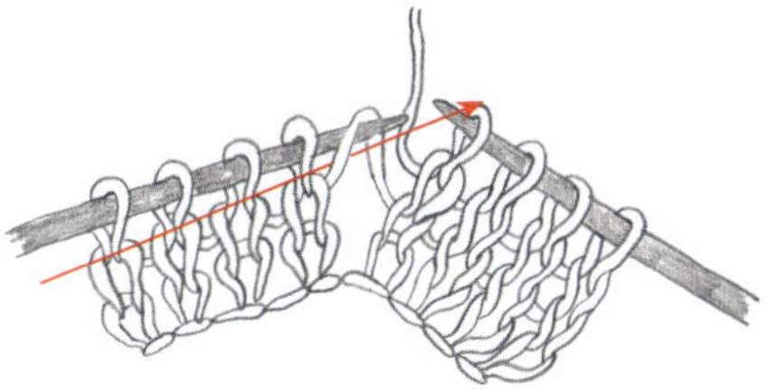

2. Knit 1 through the front loop, as shown by the arrow.

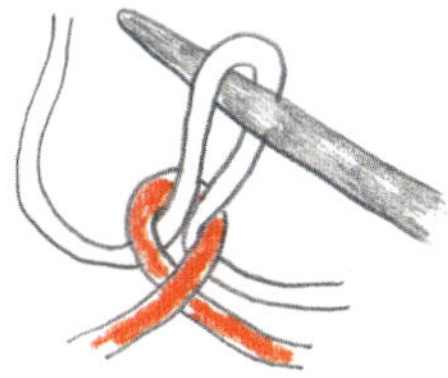

3. A new stitch slanting right has been made.

*Invisible increase in the stitch below (M1B)*

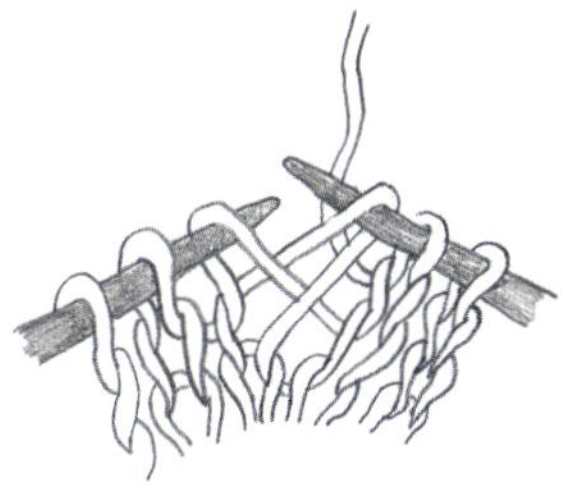

1. Insert the right needle into the stitch below the next stitch on the left hand side. Pick up the stitch and place on the left needle.

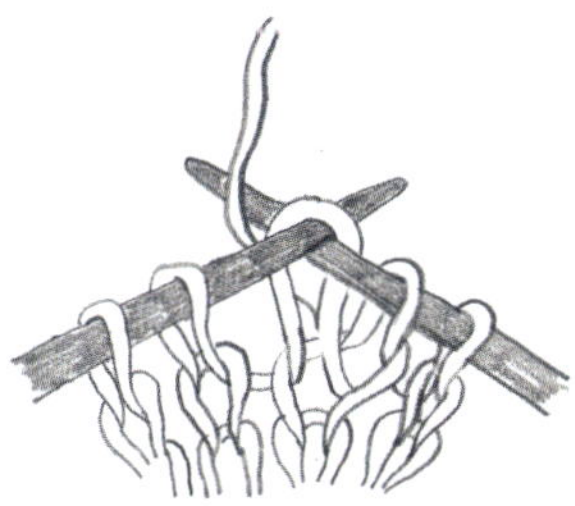

2. Knit 1 through the front loop of the new stitch, and then knit 1 in the original stitch.

### LATVIAN BRAID

ROW 1: *K1 with colour 1, k1 with colour 2*, repeat from *–* to end of row.

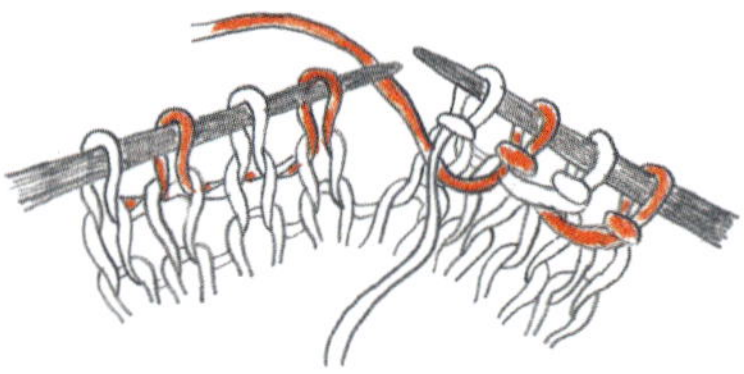

ROW 2: *P1 with colour 1, p1 with colour 2*, repeat from *–* to end of row. N.B. Hold both threads at the front of the work when you knit. For every colour change, the new yarn should be passed underneath the yarn that you have just knitted with.

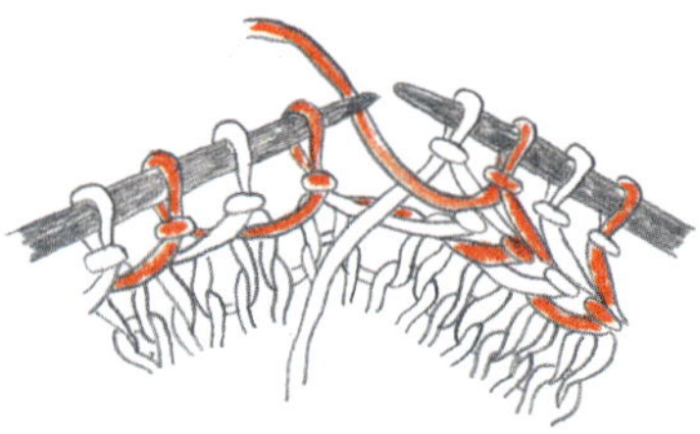

ROW 3: *P1 with colour 1, p1 with colour 2*, repeat from *–* to end of row. N.B. Hold both threads at the front of the work when you knit. For every colour change, the new yarn should be passed underneath the yarn that you have just knitted with.

### JOINING WITH KITCHENER STITCH

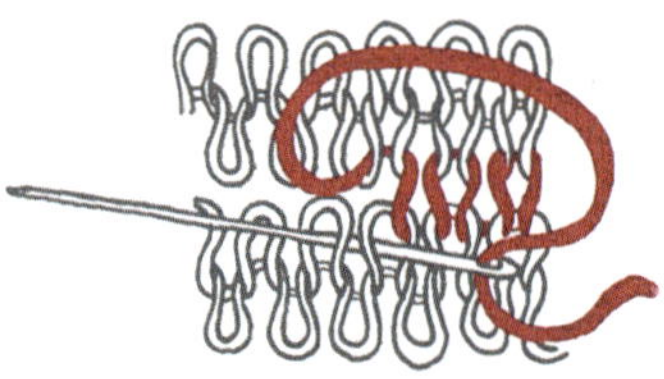

When you sew two parts together using kitchener stitch you get an invisible seam. The stitches disappear into the knitted structure without any bulky seams appearing.

### THREE NEEDLE CAST OFF

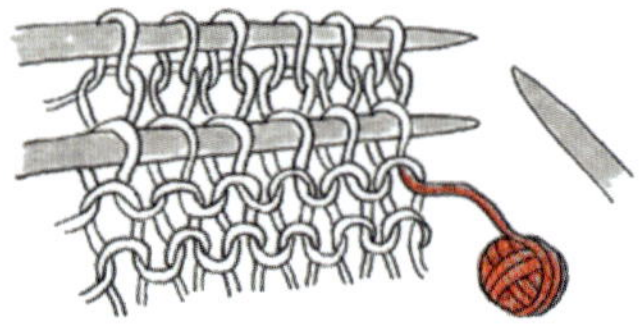

1. Cut the yarn, but leave a length to cast off with. Divide the stitches over 2 needles. Place the right sides facing each other so that the wrong sides are facing outwards. Place the needles parallel to each other.

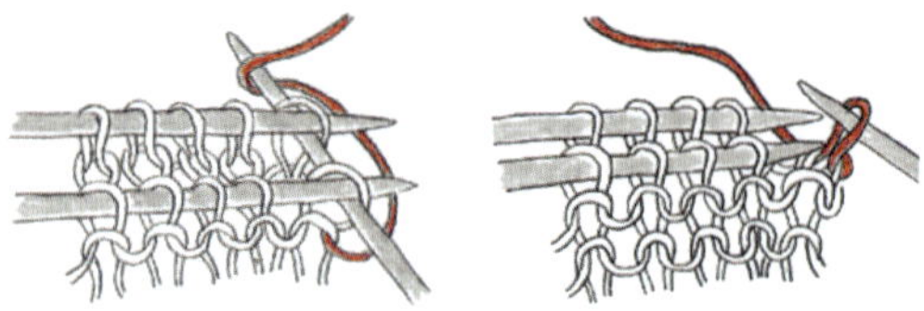

2–3. K1 through 2 sts (= 1 st from each needle).

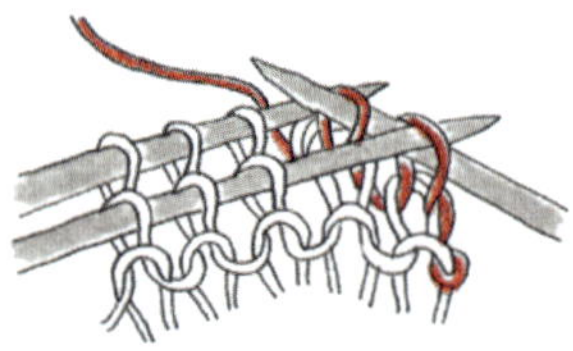

4. K1 through 2 sts.

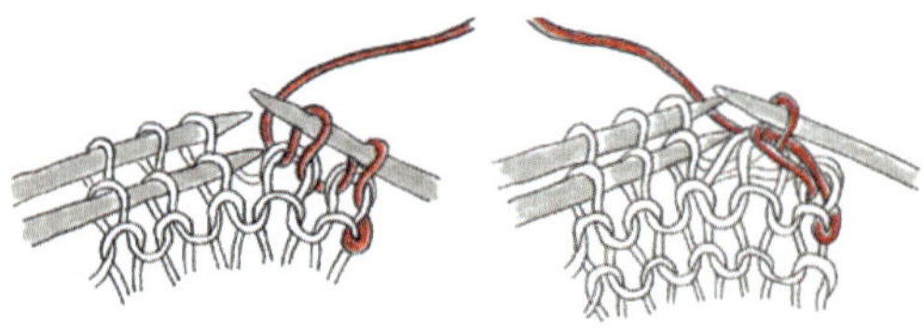

5–6. Pass the stitch that you knitted first over the second stitch. Repeat steps 4–6 until all stitches have been cast off.

### VIDEO LINKS

Instructional videos for certain techniques:
Double twisted loop technique = www.bit.ly/3xjjdCs
Italian cast on = www.bit.ly/3O8ywVg
Italian cast off = www.bit.ly/3zz3rGj
Judy's magic cast on = www.bit.ly/3Vuh5VR
Liksidig uppläggning: www.bit.ly/45kizFC
Liksidig avmaskning: www.bit.ly/3VyN2w3

# Gallery

Here you get an overview of all the knitting projects in the book, sorted by garment type. It's a nice way to choose what you what to knit, at the same time as you get the chance to browse the different designs. And perhaps even make a wishlist of the garments you dream about making?

The images show the garments lying flat, which means that you can easily see how each pattern is constructed and how the designs differ from each other. I recommend that you use these images as a starting point while you knit, since the details and patterns show up extra clear here.

If you want to combine several garments into one outfit, these spreads are perfect to leaf through in order to create your own unique winter wardrobe.

FIMBUL, PAGE 47

TUNDRA, PAGE 135

ARCTIC, PAGE 61

SISTERHOOD, PAGE 129

TUNDRA, PAGE 136

ARCTIC, PAGE 64

FORNE, PAGE 117

MICHAELMAS, PAGE 39

CHRISTMAS DAY, PAGE 87

FURA, PAGE 77

WOLF WINTER, PAGE 143

ADVENT, PAGE 53

CHRISTMAS TREE, PAGE 73

SHEAF, PAGE 103

NORE, PAGE 43

MAJA'S MAMELUCKER, PAGE 93

ARCTIC, PAGE 61

JANUARY, PAGE 139

JUNIPER, PAGE 107

FORNE, PAGE 115

LUCIA, PAGE 67

LOVE, PAGE 147

BORE, PAGE 97

BORE, PAGE 97

WINTER ROSE, PAGE 81

BLACK MAGIC, PAGE 121

*My warmest thanks to*

Helén – for magical photographs, and as always, an inspiring collaboration – without you, there wouldn't be a book!
Sebastian – for perfect design, clever solutions and a fun collaboration!
Annika – for a great deal of knowledge, support and patience through the whole process! It means so much.
Eva – for a rewarding and reliable collaboration, as usual. I am so pleased that we could make this book together – and grateful for all the help and support you give me!
Heléne – for fact checking and valuable comments!
Bonnier Fakta, my wonderful publisher – for believing in this book idea!

MODELS
Anna Karlsson
Greta Nolgård
Emma Petersson
Franka Sjöström

ANIMALS
Jeanette – for lending us your beautiful horse, Quiera Nobleza.
Lydia – for arriving with the friendly Siberians, Freya and Samson.

PROPS
Sofia Vusir Jansson – for lending us the outstandingly beautiful paper flowers!
Mia Högelin – for the fabulous illustration that you made of me knitting!

PHOTO LOCATIONS
Järvsö Local Heritage Society – for lending us the beautiful Karlsgården.
Antiqua (Antiquarian)

MAKEUP & HAIR
Michelle Vallin
Kristin Good

KNITTERS
Pernilla Olesen (Winter Rose and Lucia)
Lillemor Elfgren (Forne jumper and Sisterhood)
Ellen Furderer (Maja's mamelucker)

YARN
Lydias garn – for yarn, buttons, encouragement and all the other useful things you contribute with!

*I would also like to thank*
Ivar, Fredrika & Kerstin C
Mum, dad & Lisa
Daniel & Greta
Family, friends & colleagues
Knitters, readers & followers
Nordells café (where I wrote large parts of this book)

*And finally*: This book is dedicated to my beloved daughter Greta!

For more inspiration and knitting tips follow me on Instagram: @majasmanufaktur. There you can also ask questions about the cardigans in the book.

Have you knitted something from the book? Share it on social media with the hashtag #NordicWinterKnits.

Knit together in the Facebook group *Koftor, Sockor* and *Vantar med Maja.*

For ERRATA see:
https://www.ravelry.com/patterns/sources/vinterstickat

First published in the United Kingdom
in English by
Batsford
43 Great Ormond Street
London
WC1N 3HZ

An imprint of B. T. Batsford Holdings Limited

Translation copyright © B. T. Batsford Ltd, 2026
Copyright © Maja Karlsson, 2024

Text: Maja Karlsson
Photography: Helén Pe
Graphic design: Sebastian Wadsted
Illustrations: Siri Carlén, except 'Joining with kitchener stitch' on p160, by Katy Kimbell
Original title: Vinterstickat

First published by Bonnier Fakta, 2024, Stockholm, Sweden
Published in the English language by arrangement with Bonnier Rights, Stockholm, Sweden

All rights reserved. No part of this publication may be copied, displayed, extracted, reproduced, utilized, stored in a retrieval system or transmitted in any form or by any means, electronic, mechanical or otherwise including but not limited to photocopying, recording, or scanning without the prior written permission of the publishers.

ISBN 978 1 837 33055 3

A CIP catalogue record for this book is available from the British Library.

10 9 8 7 6 5 4 3 2 1

Reproduction by Rival Colour Ltd, UK
Printed by Toppan Leefung Printing International Ltd, China

This book can be ordered direct from the publisher at www.batsfordbooks.com, or try your local bookshop.

Distributed throughout the UK and Europe by Abrams & Chronicle Books, 1st Floor, 22–24 Ely Place, London EC1N 6TE and 57 rue Gaston Tessier, 75166 Paris, France.

www.abramsandchronicle.co.uk
info@abramsandchronicle.co.uk

FSC www.fsc.org
MIX
Paper | Supporting responsible forestry
FSC® C104723